YOUR PERSO
HO

TAURUS

Your Personal Horoscope 2017

♉

Taurus

21st April–21st May

igloobooks

igloobooks

Published in 2016
by Igloo Books Ltd
Cottage Farm
Sywell
NN6 0BJ
www.igloobooks.com

Produced for Igloo Books by Foulsham Publishing Ltd, The Old Barrel Store,
Drayman's Lane, Marlow, Bucks SL7 2FF, England

FIR003 0716
2 4 6 8 10 9 7 5 3 1
ISBN: 978-1-78557-897-7

This is an abridged version of material originally published
in Old Moore's Horoscope and Astral Diary.

Cover images: iStock
Cover designed by Nicholas Gage

Printed and manufactured in China

CONTENTS

INTRODUCTION

Your Personal Horoscopes have been specifically created to allow you to get the most from astrological patterns and the way they have a bearing on not only your zodiac sign, but nuances within it. Using the diary section of the book you can read about the influences and possibilities of each and every day of the year. It will be possible for you to see when you are likely to be cheerful and happy or those times when your nature is in retreat and you will be more circumspect. The diary will help to give you a feel for the specific 'cycles' of astrology and the way they can subtly change your day-to-day life. For example, when you see the sign ☿, this means that the planet Mercury is retrograde at that time. Retrograde means it appears to be running backwards through the zodiac. Such a happening has a significant effect on communication skills, but this is only one small aspect of how the Personal Horoscope can help you.

With Your Personal Horoscope the story doesn't end with the diary pages. It includes simple ways for you to work out the zodiac sign the Moon occupied at the time of your birth, and what this means for your personality. In addition, if you know the time of day you were born, it is possible to discover your Ascendant, yet another important guide to your personal make-up and potential.

Many readers are interested in relationships and in knowing how well they get on with people of other astrological signs. You might also be interested in the way you appear to very different sorts of individuals. If you are such a person, the section on Venus will be of particular interest. Despite the rapidly changing position of this planet, you can work out your Venus sign, and learn what bearing it will have on your life.

Using Your Personal Horoscope you can travel on one of the most fascinating and rewarding journeys that anyone can take – the journey to a better realisation of self.

THE ESSENCE OF TAURUS

Exploring the Personality of Taurus the Bull

(21ST APRIL–21ST MAY)

What's in a sign?

Taurus is probably one of the most misunderstood signs of the zodiac. Astrologers from the past described those born under the sign of the Bull as being gentle, artistic, stubborn and refined. All of this is quite true, but there is so much more to Taureans and the only reason it isn't always discussed as much as it should be is because of basic Taurean reserve. Taureans are generally modest, and don't tend to assert themselves in a direct sense, unless in self-defence. As a result the sign is often sidelined, if not ignored.

You know what you want from life and are quite willing to work long and hard to get it. However, Taurus is also a great lover of luxury, so when circumstances permit you can be slow, ponderous and even lax. If there is a paradox here it is merely typical of Venus-ruled Taurus. On differing occasions you can be chatty or quiet, bold or timorous, smart or scruffy. It all depends on your commitment to a situation. When you are inspired there is nobody powerful enough to hold you back and when you are passionate you have the proclivities of a Casanova!

There are aspects of your nature that seldom change. For example, you are almost always friendly and approachable, and invariably have a sense of what feels and looks just right. You are capable and can work with your hands as well as your brain. You don't particularly care for dirt or squalid surroundings, preferring cleanliness, and you certainly don't take kindly to abject poverty. Most Taureans prefer the country to the coast, find loving relationships easy to deal with and are quite committed to home and family.

Whilst variety is the spice of life to many zodiac signs this is not necessarily the case for Taurus. Many people born under the sign of the Bull remain happy to occupy a specific position for years on end. It has been suggested, with more than a grain of truth, that the only thing that can get the Bull moving on occasions is a strategically placed bomb. What matters most, and which shows regularly in your dealings with the world at large, is your innate kindness and your desire to help others.

Taurus resources

The best word to describe Taurean subjects who are working to the best of their ability would be 'practical'. Nebulous situations, where you have to spend long hours thinking things through in a subconscious manner, don't suit you half as much as practical tasks, no matter how complex these might be. If you were to find yourself cast up on a desert island you would have all the necessities of life sorted out in a flash. This is not to suggest that you always recognise this potential in yourself. The problem here is that a very definite lack of self-belief is inclined to make you think that almost anyone else in the world has the edge when it comes to talent.

Another of your greatest resources is your creative potential. You always have the knack of knowing what looks and feels just right. This is as true when it comes to decorating your home as it is regarding matters out there in the big, wide world. If this skill could be allied to confidence on a regular basis, there would be little or nothing to stop you. You may well possess specific skills which others definitely don't have, and you get on best when these are really needed.

Taureans don't mind dealing with routine matters and you have a good administrative ability in a number of different fields. With a deeply intuitive streak (when you are willing to recognise it), it isn't usually hard for you to work out how any particular individual would react under given circumstances. Where you fall down on occasions is that you don't always recognise the great advantages that are yours for the taking, and self-belief could hardly be considered the Taurean's greatest virtue.

Taurus people are good at making lists, even if these are of the mental variety. Your natural warmth makes it possible for you to find friends where others would not, and the sort of advice that you offer is considered and sensible. People feel they can rely on you, a fact that could prove to be one of the most important of your resources. There is nothing at all wrong with using this ability to feather your own nest, particularly since you are not the sort of person who would willingly stand on those around you in order to get where you want to go.

Beneath the surface

To say that you are deep would be a definite understatement. Only you know how far down into the basement some of your considerations and emotions actually go. Because you exhibit a generally practical face to the world at large the true scope of the Taurean mind remains something of a mystery to those around you. Certainly you seem to be uncomplicated and even a little superficial at times, though nothing could be further from the truth. Very little happens to you that fails to be filed away in some recess or other of that great interior that is your mind's library. It may be because of this that Taurus is well known for being able to bear a grudge for a long time. However, what is sometimes forgotten is that you never let a kindness from someone else go without reward, even though it may take you a very long time to find a way to say thank you.

Affairs of the heart are of special importance to you and ties of the romantic kind go as deep as any emotion. Once you love you tend to do so quite unconditionally. It takes months or years of upsets to shake your faith in love, and it's a fact that even in these days of marital splits, Taureans are far more likely than most signs of the zodiac to remain hitched. The simple fact is that you believe in loyalty, absolutely and irrevocably. The thought of letting anyone down once you have given your word is almost unthinkable and if such a situation does occur there are almost always quite definite mitigating factors.

Rules and regulations are easy for you to deal with because you have a natural tendency to order. You are also fairly good at dealing with routines and probably have your own life well sorted out as a result. A word of caution is necessary only when this internal need for order extends too much into your external life. Taureans can be fanatical about having a tidy house or for making things work out exactly as they would wish in a work sense. These tendencies start within the recesses of your own, often closed, mind. The way forward here is to throw open the doors and windows now and again and to let those around you know how you function internally. It isn't easy, because you are quite a closed book at heart. However the exercise is well worthwhile and the results can be quite breathtaking.

Making the best of yourself

Anyone who wants to work to the best of their ability first needs a good deal of self-knowledge. In your case this means recognising just what you are capable of doing and then concentrating in these directions. Of course it's only human nature to be all the things we are not, but this tendency runs deeper in you than it does in the majority of individuals. Use your natural kindness to the full and ally this to your practical ability to get things done. Sorting things out is easy for you, so easy in fact that you sometimes fail to realise that not everyone has these skills to the same extent.

Confidence definitely seems to be evident in the way you deal with the world at large. Of course you know that this often isn't the case, but that doesn't matter. It's the way the world at large views you that counts, so keep moving forward, even on those occasions when you are shaking inside. Use your naturally creative skills to the full and cultivate that innate sense of order in ways that benefit you and the world at a very practical level.

Avoid the tendency to be stubborn by convincing yourself that so many things 'simply don't matter'. An inability to move, simply because you feel annoyed or aggrieved, is certainly going to be more of a hindrance than a help – though there are occasions when, like all facets of nature, it's essential. Cultivate the more cheerful qualities that are endemic to your nature and be prepared to mix freely with as many different sorts of people as you possibly can. Be willing to take on new responsibilities because the more you are able to do so, the greater is your natural sense of self-worth. Stitching all these qualities together and using them to your own advantage isn't always easy, but pays handsomely in the end.

The impressions you give

This is a very interesting section as far as the sign of Taurus is concerned. The reason is very simply that you fail on so many occasions to betray the sheer depth of your own Earth-sign nature. That doesn't mean to say that you come across badly to others. On the contrary, you are probably a very popular person, except with those people who mistreat or cheat others. You have a great sense of what is right, and don't tend to deviate from a point of view once you've come to terms with it.

The world sees you as capable, cheerful and generally active, though with a tendency to be sluggish and lethargic on occasions. Perhaps Taurus needs to explain itself more because even when you are not at your most vibrant best there are invariably reasons. You can be quite secretive, though only usually about yourself. This can make life with the Taurean something of a guessing game on occasions. Certainly you appear to be much more fixed in your attitude than might often be the case. Why should this be so? It's mainly because you do have extremely definite ideas about specific matters, and since you sometimes display these it's natural that others pigeon-hole you as a very 'definite' sort. Actually this is far from being the whole truth but, once again, if you don't explain yourself, others can be left in the dark.

You almost certainly are not short of friends. People recognise that you are friendly, tolerant and extremely supportive. You give the impression of being very trustworthy and people know that they can rely on you to act in a specific manner. If this appears to make you somewhat predictable it doesn't really matter because you are deeply loved, and that's what counts. One fact is almost certain – the world has a greater regard for you in a general sense than you have for yourself.

The way forward

The ideal life for the Taurus subject seems to be one that is settled and happy, with not too much upheaval and plenty of order. Whether or not this truly turns out to be the case depends on a number of factors. For starters, even those born under the sign of the Bull have a boredom threshold. This means that having to respond to change and diversity probably does you more good than you might at first think. At the same time you won't know exactly what you are capable of doing unless you really stretch yourself, and that's something that you are not always willing to do.

You do function best from within loving relationships, and although you can be very passionate, once you have given your heart you don't tend to change your mind readily. Personal and domestic contentment are worth a great deal to you because they represent the platform upon which you build the rest of your life. You don't make a good itinerant and probably won't indulge in travel for its own sake. Of course it does you good to get around, since anything that broadens your horizons has got to be an advantage, but you'll probably always maintain a solid home base and relish the prospect of coming back to it as frequently as possible.

Most Taureans are family people. You can be a capable parent, though tend to be a little more authoritarian than some types. Keeping an ordered sort of life is at the base of your psychology, so that even when you are young and less tidy-minded there is always a basic desire for self-discipline. This often extends to your work, where you are extremely capable and can quite easily work under your own supervision. You recognise the beautiful in all spheres of life and tend to gravitate towards clean and sanitary surroundings.

In matters of health you tend to be fairly robust, though you can suffer somewhat with headaches, often brought about as a result of a stiff neck and stress. This latter is what you should avoid as much as possible. Saying what you feel, and listening carefully to the responses, is definitely of great importance. The more you learn, the wiser you become. This makes you the natural resort of others when they need help and advice. If you try not to underestimate your own abilities, you can rise as far in life as the world at large thinks you are capable of doing. At the end of the day it is important to recognise your popularity. In all probability your friends have a much higher opinion of you than the one you cultivate for yourself.

TAURUS ON THE CUSP

Astrological profiles are altered for those people born at either the beginning or the end of a zodiac sign, or, more properly, on the cusps of a sign. In the case of Taurus this would be on the 21st of April and for two or three days after, and similarly at the end of the sign, probably from the 18th to the 21st of May.

The Aries Cusp – 21st to 24th April

Although you have all the refinement, breeding and creative flair of the true Taurean, you are definitely more of a go-getter. Knowing what you want from life there is a slight possibility that you might be accused of being bossy and sometimes this slightly hurts your Taurean sensitivity. You have plenty of energy to get through the things that you see as being important but it is quite possible that those around you don't always see things in the same light, and this can be annoying to you. Like the typical Taurean you have great reserves of energy and can work long and hard towards any particular objective although, because Aries is also in attendance, you may push yourself slightly harder than is strictly necessary. Your temper is variable and you may not always display the typical Taurean patience with those around you.

It is possible for Taurus to 'wait in the wings' deliberately and therefore to lose out on some of the most important potential gains as a result. In your case, this is much less likely. You don't worry too much about speaking your mind. You are loving and kind, but even family members know that they will only be able to push you so far. At work, you are capable and have executive ability. Like the Taurean you don't really care for getting your hands dirty, but if needs must you can pitch in with the best of them and enjoy a challenge. You don't worry as much as some of your Taurean friends do, but all the same you regularly expect too much of your nervous system and need frequent periods of rest.

Try not to impose your will on those around you and be content to allow things to happen on their own sometimes. This might not be an easy thing for the Aries-cusp Taurean but it's one of the sure ways to success. Confidence isn't lacking and neither is basic patience, but they do have to be encouraged and nurtured.

The Gemini Cusp – 18th to 21st May

Oh, what a happy person you are – and how much the world loves you for it! This is definitely the more potentially fortunate of the two Taurean cusps, or at least that is how the majority of the people who know you would view it. The fact is that you are bright and breezy, easygoing and sometimes fickle on occasions, but supporting these trends is a patient, generally contented attitude to life that is both refreshing and inspiring. Getting others on your side is not hard and you have plenty of energy when it is needed the most. All the same you are quite capable of dozing in the sun occasionally and probably put far less stress on your nervous system than either Taurus or Gemini when taken alone.

You don't care too much for routines and you love variety, but yet you retain the creative and artistic qualities that come with the sign of the Bull. You work well and with confidence, but would be very likely to change direction in your career at some stage in your life and are not half so tied to routine as is usually the case for Taurus. With a friendly, and even a passionate, approach to matters of the heart you are an attentive lover and a fond parent. Most people know what you really are because you are only too willing to show them. Working out the true motivations that lurk within your soul is part of your personal search to know 'self' and is extremely important.

All in all, you have exactly what it takes to get on in life and a sense of joy and fun that makes you good to know. Patience balances your need to 'get going', whilst your mischievous streak lightens the load of the sign of Taurus which can, on occasions, take itself rather more seriously than it should.

There are many ways of coping with the requirements of life and, at one time or another, it is likely that you will try them all out. But above and beyond your need to experiment you know what is most important to you and that will always be your ultimate goal. What matters the most is your smile, which is enduring and even alluring.

TAURUS AND ITS ASCENDANTS

The nature of every individual on the planet is composed of the rich variety of zodiac signs and planetary positions that were present at the time of their birth. Your Sun sign, which in your case is Taurus, is one of the many factors when it comes to assessing the unique person you are. Probably the most important consideration, other than your Sun sign, is to establish the zodiac sign that was rising over the eastern horizon at the time that you were born. This is your Ascending or Rising sign. Most popular astrology fails to take account of the Ascendant, and yet its importance remains with you from the very moment of your birth, through every day of your life. The Ascendant is evident in the way you approach the world, and so, when meeting a person for the first time, it is this astrological influence that you are most likely to notice first. Our Ascending sign essentially represents what we appear to be, while the Sun sign is what we feel inside ourselves.

The Ascendant also has the potential for modifying our overall nature. For example, if you were born at a time of day when Taurus was passing over the eastern horizon (this would be around the time of dawn) then you would be classed as a double Taurus. As such, you would typify this zodiac sign, both internally and in your dealings with others. However, if your Ascendant sign turned out to be a Fire sign, such as Leo, there would be a profound alteration of nature, away from the expected qualities of Taurus.

One of the reasons why popular astrology often ignores the Ascendant is that it has always been rather difficult to establish. We have found a way to make this possible by devising an easy-to-use table, which you will find on page 157 of this book. Using this, you can establish your Ascendant sign at a glance. You will need to know your rough time of birth, then it is simply a case of following the instructions.

For those readers who have no idea of their time of birth it might be worth allowing a good friend, or perhaps your partner, to read through the section that follows this introduction. Someone who deals with you on a regular basis may easily discover your Ascending sign, even though you could have some difficulty establishing it for yourself. A good understanding of this component of your nature is essential if you want to be aware of that 'other person' who is responsible for the way you make contact with the world at large. Your Sun sign, Ascendant sign, and the other pointers in this book will, together, allow you a far better understanding of what makes you tick as an individual. Peeling back the different layers of your astrological make-up can be an enlightening experience, and the Ascendant may represent one of the most important layers of all.

Taurus with Taurus Ascendant

The world would see you as being fairly typical of the sign of Taurus, so you are careful, sensitive, well bred and, if other astrological trends agree, very creative. Nothing pleases you more than a tidy environment to live in and a peaceful life. You probably believe that there is a place for everything and will do your best to keep it all where it should be. It's a pity that this sometimes includes people, and you are certain to get rather irritated if they don't behave in the way that you would expect. Despite this, you are generally understanding and are very capable of giving and receiving affection.

Not everyone knows the real you, however, and it is sometimes difficult to tell the world those most personal details that can be locked deep inside. At an emotional level you tend to idealise love somewhat, though if anything this presents itself to the world as a slight 'coldness' on occasions. This is far from the truth, but your tidy mind demands that even the most intimate processes are subjected to the same sense of order with which you view the world at large. Unlike many sign combinations, you don't really rely on the help and support of others because you are more than capable yourself. In the main you live a happy life and have the ability to pass on this trait to those you care for.

Taurus with Gemini Ascendant

This is a generally happy combination which finds you better able to externalise the cultured and creative qualities which are inherent in your Taurean nature. You love to be around interesting and stimulating people and tend to be much more talkative than the typical Taurean is expected to be. The reason why Gemini helps here is because it lightens the load somewhat. Taurus is not the most introspective sign of the zodiac, but it does have that quality, and a good dose of Gemini allows you to speak your mind more freely and, as a result, to know yourself better too.

Although your mind tends to be fairly logical, you also enjoy flashes of insight that can cause you to behave in a less rational way from time to time. This is probably no bad thing because life will never be boring with you around. You try to convince yourself that you take on board all the many and varied opinions that come back at you from others, though there is a slight danger of intellectual snobbery if the responses you get are not the expected ones. You particularly like clean houses, funny people and probably fast cars. Financial rewards can come thick and fast to the Gemini-Ascendant Taurean when the logical but inspirational mind is harnessed to practical matters.

Taurus with Cancer Ascendant

Your main aim in life seems to be to look after everyone and everything that you come across. From your deepest and most enduring human love, right down to the birds in the park, you really do care and you show that natural affection in a thousand different ways. Your nature is sensitive and you are easily moved to tears, though this does not prevent you from pitching in and doing practical things to assist at just about any level. There is a danger that you could stifle those same people whom you set out to assist, and people with this zodiac combination are often unwilling, or unable, to allow their children to grow and leave the nest. More time spent considering what suits you would be no bad thing, but the problem is that you find it almost impossible to imagine any situation that doesn't involve your most basic need, which is to nurture.

You appear not to possess a selfish streak, though it sometimes turns out that, in being certain that you understand the needs and wants of the world, you are nevertheless treading on their toes. This eventual realisation can be very painful, but it isn't a stick with which you should beat yourself because at heart you are one of the kindest people imaginable. Your sense of fair play means that you are a quiet social reformer at heart.

Taurus with Leo Ascendant

Oh dear, this can be rather a hedonistic combination. The trouble is that Taurus tends to have a great sense of what looks and feels right, whilst Leo, being a Cat, is inclined to preen itself on almost any occasion. The combination tends towards self-love, which is all too likely for someone who is perfect. But don't be too dispirited about these facts because there is a great deal going for you in other ways. For a start you have one of the warmest hearts to be found anywhere and you are so brave that others marvel at the courage you display. The mountains that you climb may not be of the large, rocky sort, but you manage to find plenty of pinnacles to scale all the same, and you invariably get to the top.

Routines might bore you a little more than would be the case with Taurus alone, but you don't mind being alone. Why should you? You are probably the nicest person you know! Thus if you were ever to be cast up on a deserted island you would people the place all on your own, and there would never be any crime, untidiness or arguments. Problems only arise when other people are involved. However, in social settings you are charming, good to know and full of ideas that really have legs. You preserve your youth well into middle age, but at base you can tend to worry more than is good for you.

Taurus with Virgo Ascendant

This combination tends to amplify the Taurean qualities that you naturally possess and this is the case because both Taurus and Virgo are Earth signs. However, there are certain factors related to Virgo that show themselves very differently than the sign's cousin Taurus. Virgo is more fussy, nervy and pedantic than Taurus and all of these qualities are going to show up in your nature at one level or another. On the plus side, you might be slightly less concerned about having a perfect home and a perfect family, and your interest in life appears at a more direct level than that of the true Taurean. You care very much about your home and family and are very loyal to your friends. It's true that you sometimes tend to try and take them over, and you can also show a marked tendency to dominate, but your heart is in the right place, and most people recognise that your caring is genuine.

One problem is that there are very few shades of grey in your life, which is certainly not the case for other zodiac sign combinations. Living your life in the way that you do, there isn't much room for compromise, and this fact alone can prove to be something of a problem where relationships are concerned. In a personal sense you need a partner who is willing to be organised and one who relies heavily on your judgements, which don't change very often.

Taurus with Libra Ascendant

A fortunate combination in many ways, this is a double Venus rulership, since both Taurus and Libra are heavily reliant on the planet of love. You are social, amiable and a natural diplomat, anxious to please and ready to care for just about anyone who shows interest in you. You hate disorder, which means that there is a place for everything and everything in its place. This can throw up the odd paradox, however, since being half Libran you cannot always work out where that place ought to be! You deal with life in a humorous way and are quite capable of seeing the absurd in yourself, as well as in others. Your heart is no bigger than that of the dyed-in-the-wool Taurean, but it sits rather closer to the surface and so others recognise it more.

On those occasions when you know you are standing on firm ground you can show great confidence, even if you have to be ready to change some of your opinions at the drop of a hat. When this happens you can be quite at odds with yourself, because Taurus doesn't take very many U-turns, whereas Libra does. Don't expect to know yourself too well, and keep looking for the funny side of things, because it is within humour that you forge the sort of life that suits you best.

Taurus with Scorpio Ascendant

The first, last and most important piece of advice for you is not to take yourself, or anyone else, too seriously. This might be rather a tall order because Scorpio intensifies the deeper qualities of Taurus and can make you rather lacking in the sense of humour that we all need to live our lives in this most imperfect of worlds. You are naturally sensuous by nature. This shows itself in a host of ways. In all probability you can spend hours in the bath, love to treat yourself to good food and drink and take your greatest pleasure in neat and orderly surroundings. On occasions this can alienate you from those who live in the same house, because other people do need to use the bathroom from time to time, and they cannot remain tidy indefinitely.

You tend to worry a great deal about things which are really not very important, but don't take this statement too seriously or you will begin to worry about this, too! You often need to lighten up and should always do your best to tell yourself that most things are not half so important as they seem to be. Be careful over the selection of a life partner and if possible choose someone who is naturally funny and who does not take life anywhere near as seriously as you are inclined to do. At work you are more than capable and in all probability everyone relies heavily on your wise judgements.

Taurus with Sagittarius Ascendant

A dual nature is evident here, and if it doesn't serve to confuse you, it will certainly be a cause of concern to many of the people with whom you share your life. You like to have a good time and are a natural party-goer. On such occasions you are accommodating, chatty and good to know. But contrast this with the quieter side of Taurus, which is directly opposed to your Sagittarian qualities. The opposition of forces is easy for you to deal with because you inhabit your own body and mind all the time, but it's far less easy for friends and relatives to understand. So on those occasions when you decide that, socially speaking, enough is enough, you may have trouble explaining this to the twelve people who are waiting outside your door with party hats and whoopee cushions.

Confidence to do almost anything is not far from the forefront of your mind and you readily embark on adventures that would have some types flapping about in horror. Here again, it is important to realise that we are not all built the same way and that gentle coaxing is sometimes necessary to bring others round to your point of view. If you really have a fault it could be that you are so busy being your own, rather less than predictable self, that you fail to take the rest of the world into account.

Taurus with Capricorn Ascendant

It might appear on the surface that you are not the most interesting person in the world. This is a pity, for you have an active though very logical mind, so logical in some instances that you would have a great deal in common with Mr Spock. This is the thorn in your flesh, or rather the flesh of everyone else, since you are probably quite happy being exactly what you are. You can think things through in a clear and very practical way and end up taking decisions that are balanced, eminently sensible, but, on occasions, rather dull.

Actually there is a fun machine somewhere deep within that Earth-sign nature and those who know you the best will recognise the fact. Often this combination is attended by a deep and biting sense of humour, but it's of the sort that less intelligent and considered types would find rather difficult to recognise. It is likely that you have no lack of confidence in your own judgement and you have all the attributes necessary to do very well on the financial front. Slow and steady progress is your way and you need to be quite certain before you commit yourself to any new venture. This is a zodiac combination that can soak up years of stress and numerous difficulties, yet still come out on top. Nothing holds you back for long and you tend to be very brave.

Taurus with Aquarius Ascendant

There is nothing that you fail to think about deeply and with great intensity. You are wise, honest and very scientific in your approach to life. Routines are necessary in life, but you have most of them sorted out well in advance and so always have time to look at the next interesting fact. If you don't spend all your time watching documentaries on the television set, you make a good friend and love to socialise. Most of the great discoveries of the world were probably made by people with this sort of astrological combination, though your nature is rather 'odd' on occasions and so can be rather difficult for others to understand.

You may be most surprised when others tell you that you are eccentric, but you don't really mind too much because for half of the time you are not inhabiting the same world as the rest of us. Because you can be delightfully dotty you are probably much loved and cherished by your friends, of which there are likely to be many. Family members probably adore you too and you can be guaranteed to entertain anyone with whom you come into contact. The only fly in the ointment is that you sometimes lose track of reality, whatever that might be, and fly high in your own atmosphere of rarefied possibilities.

Taurus with Pisces Ascendant

You are clearly a very sensitive type of person and that sometimes makes it rather difficult for others to know how they might best approach you. Private and deep, you are nevertheless socially inclined on many occasions. However, because your nature is bottomless it is possible that some types would actually accuse you of being shallow. How can this come about? Well, it's simple really. The fact is that you rarely show anyone what is going on in the deepest recesses of your mind and so your responses can appear to be trite or even ill-considered. This is far from the truth, as those who are allowed into the 'inner sanctum' would readily admit. You are something of a sensualist, and relish staying in bed late and simply pleasing yourself for days on end. However, you are a Taurean at heart so you desire a tidy environment in which to live your usually long life.

You are able to deal with the routine aspects of life quite well and can be a capable worker once you are up and firing on all cylinders. It is very important that you maintain an interest in what you are doing because the recesses of your dreamy mind can sometimes appear to be infinitely more attractive. Your imagination is second to none and this fact can often be turned to your advantage.

Taurus with Aries Ascendant

This is a steady combination, so much so that even experienced astrologers would be unlikely to recognise that the Aries quality is present at all, unless of course they came to know you very well. Your approach to life tends to be slow and considered and there is a great danger that you could suppress those feelings that others of your kind would be only too willing to verbalise. To compensate, you are deeply creative and will think matters through much more readily than more dominant Aries types would be inclined to do. In your dealings with the world, you are, nevertheless, somewhat locked inside yourself and can struggle to achieve the level of communication that you so desperately need. Frustration might follow, were it not for the fact that you possess a quiet determination that, to those in the know, is the clearest window through to your Taurean soul.

The care for others is strong and you certainly demonstrate this at all levels. The fact is that you live a great percentage of your life in service to the people you take to, whilst at the same time being able to shut the door firmly in the face of people who irritate or anger you. You are deeply motivated towards family relationships.

THE MOON AND THE PART IT PLAYS IN YOUR LIFE

In astrology the Moon is probably the single most important heavenly body after the Sun. Its unique position, as partner to the Earth on its journey around the solar system, means that the Moon appears to pass through the signs of the zodiac extremely quickly. The zodiac position of the Moon at the time of your birth plays a great part in personal character and is especially significant in the build-up of your emotional nature.

Your Own Moon Sign

Discovering the position of the Moon at the time of your birth has always been notoriously difficult because tracking the complex zodiac positions of the Moon is not easy. This process has been reduced to three simple stages with our Lunar Tables. A breakdown of the Moon's zodiac positions can be found from page 35 onwards, so that once you know what your Moon Sign is, you can see what part this plays in the overall build-up of your personal character.

If you follow the instructions on the next page you will soon be able to work out exactly what zodiac sign the Moon occupied on the day that you were born and you can then go on to compare the reading for this position with those of your Sun sign and your Ascendant. It is partly the comparison between these three important positions that goes towards making you the unique individual you are.

HOW TO DISCOVER YOUR MOON SIGN

This is a three-stage process. You may need a pen and a piece of paper but if you follow the instructions below the process should only take a minute or so.

STAGE 1 First of all you need to know the Moon Age at the time of your birth. If you look at Moon Table 1, on page 33, you will find all the years between 1919 and 2017 down the left side. Find the year of your birth and then trace across to the right to the month of your birth. Where the two intersect you will find a number. This is the date of the New Moon in the month that you were born. You now need to count forward the number of days between the New Moon and your own birthday. For example, if the New Moon in the month of your birth was shown as being the 6th and you were born on the 20th, your Moon Age Day would be 14. If the New Moon in the month of your birth came after your birthday, you need to count forward from the New Moon in the previous month. Whatever the result, jot this number down so that you do not forget it.

STAGE 2 Take a look at Moon Table 2 on page 34. Down the left hand column look for the date of your birth. Now trace across to the month of your birth. Where the two meet you will find a letter. Copy this letter down alongside your Moon Age Day.

STAGE 3 Moon Table 3 on page 34 will supply you with the zodiac sign the Moon occupied on the day of your birth. Look for your Moon Age Day down the left hand column and then for the letter you found in Stage 2. Where the two converge you will find a zodiac sign and this is the sign occupied by the Moon on the day that you were born.

Your Zodiac Moon Sign Explained

You will find a profile of all zodiac Moon Signs on pages 35 to 38, showing in yet another way how astrology helps to make you into the individual that you are. In each daily entry of the Astral Diary you can find the zodiac position of the Moon for every day of the year. This also allows you to discover your lunar birthdays. Since the Moon passes through all the signs of the zodiac in about a month, you can expect something like twelve lunar birthdays each year. At these times you are likely to be emotionally steady and able to make the sort of decisions that have real, lasting value.

MOON TABLE 1

YEAR	MAR	APR	MAY	YEAR	MAR	APR	MAY	YEAR	MAR	APR	MAY
1919	2/31	30	29	1952	25	24	23	1985	21	20	19
1920	20	18	18	1953	15	13	13	1986	10	9	8
1921	9	8	7	1954	5	3	2	1987	29	28	27
1922	28	27	26	1955	24	22	21	1988	18	16	15
1923	17	16	15	1956	12	11	10	1989	7	6	5
1924	5	4	3	1957	1/31	29	29	1990	26	25	24
1925	24	23	22	1958	20	19	18	1991	15	13	13
1926	14	12	11	1959	9	8	7	1992	4	3	2
1927	3	2	1/30	1960	27	26	26	1993	24	22	21
1928	21	20	19	1961	16	15	14	1994	12	11	10
1929	11	9	9	1962	6	5	4	1995	30	29	29
1930	30	28	28	1963	25	23	23	1996	19	18	18
1931	19	18	17	1964	14	12	11	1997	9	7	6
1932	7	6	5	1965	2	1	1/30	1998	27	26	25
1933	26	24	24	1966	21	20	19	1999	17	16	15
1934	15	13	13	1967	10	9	8	2000	6	4	4
1935	5	3	2	1968	29	28	27	2001	24	23	22
1936	23	21	20	1969	18	16	15	2002	13	12	10
1937	13	12	10	1970	7	6	6	2003	2	1	1/30
1938	2/31	30	29	1971	26	25	24	2004	21	19	18
1939	20	19	19	1972	15	13	13	2005	10	8	8
1940	9	7	7	1973	5	3	2	2006	29	27	27
1941	27	26	26	1974	24	22	21	2007	18	17	15
1942	16	15	15	1975	12	11	11	2008	7	6	5
1943	6	4	4	1976	30	29	29	2009	26	25	24
1944	24	22	22	1977	19	18	18	2010	15	14	14
1945	14	12	11	1978	9	7	7	2011	5	3	3
1946	3	2	1/30	1979	27	26	26	2012	22	21	20
1947	21	20	19	1980	16	15	14	2013	12	10	10
1948	11	9	9	1981	6	4	4	2014	1/31	30	29
1949	29	28	27	1982	24	23	21	2015	20	19	18
1950	18	17	17	1983	14	13	12	2016	8	7	8
1951	7	6	6	1984	2	1	1/30	2017	27	25	25

TABLE 2

DAY	APR	MAY
1	J	M
2	J	M
3	J	M
4	J	M
5	J	M
6	J	M
7	J	M
8	J	M
9	J	M
10	J	M
11	K	M
12	K	N
13	K	N
14	K	N
15	K	N
16	K	N
17	K	N
18	K	N
19	K	N
20	K	N
21	L	N
22	L	O
23	L	O
24	L	O
25	L	O
26	L	O
27	L	O
28	L	O
29	L	O
30	L	O
31	–	O

MOON TABLE 3

M/D	J	K	L	M	N	O	P
0	AR	TA	TA	TA	GE	GE	GE
1	TA	TA	TA	GE	GE	GE	CA
2	TA	TA	GE	GE	GE	CA	CA
3	TA	GE	GE	GE	CA	CA	CA
4	GE	GE	GE	CA	CA	CA	LE
5	GE	CA	CA	CA	LE	LE	LE
6	CA	CA	CA	LE	LE	LE	VI
7	CA	CA	LE	LE	LE	VI	VI
8	CA	LE	LE	LE	VI	VI	VI
9	LE	LE	VI	VI	VI	LI	LI
10	LE	VI	VI	VI	LI	LI	LI
11	VI	VI	VI	LI	LI	SC	SC
12	VI	VI	LI	LI	LI	SC	SC
13	VI	LI	LI	LI	SC	SC	SC
14	LI	LI	LI	SC	SC	SA	SA
15	LI	SC	SC	SC	SA	SA	SA
16	SC	SC	SC	SA	SA	SA	CP
17	SC	SC	SA	SA	SA	CP	CP
18	SC	SA	SA	SA	CP	CP	CP
19	SA	SA	SA	CP	CP	CP	AQ
20	SA	CP	CP	CP	AQ	AQ	AQ
21	CP	CP	CP	AQ	AQ	AQ	PI
22	CP	CP	AQ	AQ	AQ	PI	PI
23	CP	AQ	AQ	AQ	PI	PI	PI
24	AQ	AQ	AQ	PI	PI	PI	AR
25	AQ	PI	PI	PI	AR	AR	AR
26	PI	PI	PI	AR	AR	AR	TA
27	PI	PI	AR	AR	AR	TA	TA
28	PI	AR	AR	AR	TA	TA	TA
29	AR	AR	AR	TA	TA	TA	GE

AR = Aries, TA = Taurus, GE = Gemini, CA = Cancer, LE = Leo, VI = Virgo, LI = Libra, SC = Scorpio, SA = Sagittarius, CP = Capricorn, AQ = Aquarius, PI = Pisces

MOON SIGNS

Moon in Aries

You have a strong imagination, courage, determination and a desire to do things in your own way and forge your own path through life.

Originality is a key attribute; you are seldom stuck for ideas although your mind is changeable and you could take the time to focus on individual tasks. Often quick-tempered, you take orders from few people and live life at a fast pace. Avoid health problems by taking regular time out for rest and relaxation.

Emotionally, it is important that you talk to those you are closest to and work out your true feelings. Once you discover that people are there to help, there is less necessity for you to do everything yourself.

Moon in Taurus

The Moon in Taurus gives you a courteous and friendly manner, which means you are likely to have many friends.

The good things in life mean a lot to you, as Taurus is an Earth sign that delights in experiences which please the senses. Hence you are probably a lover of good food and drink, which may in turn mean you need to keep an eye on the bathroom scales, especially as looking good is also important to you.

Emotionally you are fairly stable and you stick by your own standards. Taureans do not respond well to change. Intuition also plays an important part in your life.

Moon in Gemini

You have a warm-hearted character, sympathetic and eager to help others. At times reserved, you can also be articulate and chatty: this is part of the paradox of Gemini, which always brings duplicity to the nature. You are interested in current affairs, have a good intellect, and are good company and likely to have many friends. Most of your friends have a high opinion of you and would be ready to defend you should the need arise. However, this is usually unnecessary, as you are quite capable of defending yourself in any verbal confrontation.

Travel is important to your inquisitive mind and you find intellectual stimulus in mixing with people from different cultures. You also gain much from reading, writing and the arts but you do need plenty of rest and relaxation in order to avoid fatigue.

Moon in Cancer

The Moon in Cancer at the time of birth is a fortunate position as Cancer is the Moon's natural home. This means that the qualities of compassion and understanding given by the Moon are especially enhanced in your nature, and you are friendly and sociable and cope well with emotional pressures. You cherish home and family life, and happily do the domestic tasks. Your surroundings are important to you and you hate squalor and filth. You are likely to have a love of music and poetry.

Your basic character, although at times changeable like the Moon itself, depends on symmetry. You aim to make your surroundings comfortable and harmonious, for yourself and those close to you.

Moon in Leo

The best qualities of the Moon and Leo come together to make you warm-hearted, fair, ambitious and self-confident. With good organisational abilities, you invariably rise to a position of responsibility in your chosen career. This is fortunate as you don't enjoy being an 'also-ran' and would rather be an important part of a small organisation than a menial in a large one.

You should be lucky in love, and happy, provided you put in the effort to make a comfortable home for yourself and those close to you. It is likely that you will have a love of pleasure, sport, music and literature. Life brings you many rewards, most of them as a direct result of your own efforts, although you may be luckier than average and ready to make the best of any situation.

Moon in Virgo

You are endowed with good mental abilities and a keen receptive memory, but you are never ostentatious or pretentious. Naturally quite reserved, you still have many friends, especially of the opposite sex. Marital relationships must be discussed carefully and worked at so that they remain harmonious, as personal attachments can be a problem if you do not give them your full attention.

Talented and persevering, you possess artistic qualities and are a good homemaker. Earning your honours through genuine merit, you work long and hard towards your objectives but show little pride in your achievements. Many short journeys will be undertaken in your life.

Moon in Libra

With the Moon in Libra you are naturally popular and make friends easily. People like you, probably more than you realise, you bring fun to a party and are a natural diplomat. For all its good points, Libra is not the most stable of astrological signs and, as a result, your emotions can be a little unstable too. Therefore, although the Moon in Libra is said to be good for love and marriage, your Sun sign and Rising sign will have an important effect on your emotional and loving qualities.

You must remember to relate to others in your decision-making. Co-operation is crucial because Libra represents the 'balance' of life that can only be achieved through harmonious relationships. Conformity is not easy for you because Libra, an Air sign, likes its independence.

Moon in Scorpio

Some people might call you pushy. In fact, all you really want to do is to live life to the full and protect yourself and your family from the pressures of life. Take care to avoid giving the impression of being sarcastic or impulsive and use your energies wisely and constructively.

You have great courage and you invariably achieve your goals by force of personality and sheer effort. You are fond of mystery and are good at predicting the outcome of situations and events. Travel experiences can be beneficial to you.

You may experience problems if you do not take time to examine your motives in a relationship, and also if you allow jealousy, always a feature of Scorpio, to cloud your judgement.

Moon in Sagittarius

The Moon in Sagittarius helps to make you a generous individual with humanitarian qualities and a kind heart. Restlessness may be intrinsic as your mind is seldom still. Perhaps because of this, you have a need for change that could lead you to several major moves during your adult life. You are not afraid to stand your ground when you know your judgement is right, you speak directly and have good intuition.

At work you are quick, efficient and versatile and so you make an ideal employee. You need work to be intellectually demanding and do not enjoy tedious routines.

In relationships, you anger quickly if faced with stupidity or deception, though you are just as quick to forgive and forget. Emotionally, there are times when your heart rules your head.

Moon in Capricorn

The Moon in Capricorn makes you popular and likely to come into the public eye in some way. The watery Moon is not entirely comfortable in the Earth sign of Capricorn and this may lead to some difficulties in the early years of life. An initial lack of creative ability and indecision must be overcome before the true qualities of patience and perseverance inherent in Capricorn can show through.

You have good administrative ability and are a capable worker, and if you are careful you can accumulate wealth. But you must be cautious and take professional advice in partnerships, as you are open to deception. You may be interested in social or welfare work, which suit your organisational skills and sympathy for others.

Moon in Aquarius

The Moon in Aquarius makes you an active and agreeable person with a friendly, easy-going nature. Sympathetic to the needs of others, you flourish in a laid-back atmosphere. You are broad-minded, fair and open to suggestion, although sometimes you have an unconventional quality which others can find hard to understand.

You are interested in the strange and curious, and in old articles and places. You enjoy trips to these places and gain much from them. Political, scientific and educational work interests you and you might choose a career in science or technology.

Money-wise, you make gains through innovation and concentration and Lunar Aquarians often tackle more than one job at a time. In love you are kind and honest.

Moon in Pisces

You have a kind, sympathetic nature, somewhat retiring at times, but you always take account of others' feelings and help when you can.

Personal relationships may be problematic, but as life goes on you can learn from your experiences and develop a better understanding of yourself and the world around you.

You have a fondness for travel, appreciate beauty and harmony and hate disorder and strife. You may be fond of literature and would make a good writer or speaker yourself. You have a creative imagination and may come across as an incurable romantic. You have strong intuition, maybe bordering on a mediumistic quality, which sets you apart from the mass. You may not be rich in cash terms, but your personal gifts are worth more than gold.

TAURUS IN LOVE

Discover how compatible in love you are with people from the same and other signs of the zodiac. Five stars equals a match made in heaven!

Taurus meets Taurus

A certainty for complete success or absolute failure. Taurus has enough self-knowledge to recognise the strengths of a fellow Taurean, so these two can live in harmony. Both will be tidy and live in comfortable surroundings. Two Taureans seldom argue and will be good friends. But something may be lacking – a spark that doesn't ignite. Passion is important and Taurus reflects, rather than creates it. The prognosis is good, but someone must turn the heat up to get things really cooking. Star rating: ****

Taurus meets Gemini

Gemini people can infuriate the generally steady Taurean nature as they are so untidy, which is a complete reversal of the Taurean ethos. At first this won't matter; Mr or Miss Gemini is enchanting, entertaining and very different. But time will tell, and that's why this potential relationship only has two stars. There is hope, however, because Taurus can curb some of the excesses of the Twins, whilst Gemini is capable of preventing the Bull from taking itself too seriously. Star rating: **

Taurus meets Cancer

This pair will have the tidiest house in the street – every stick of furniture in place, and no errant blade of grass daring to spoil the lawn. But things inside the relationship might not be quite so shipshape as both signs need, but don't offer, encouragement. There's plenty of affection, but few incentives for mutual progress. This might not prevent material success, but an enduring relationship isn't based on money alone. Passion is essential, and both parties need to realise and aim for that. Star rating: **

Taurus meets Leo

Here we find a generally successful pairing, which frequently leads to an enduring relationship. Taurus needs stimulation which Leo is happy to offer, while Leo responds well to the Bull's sense of order. The essence of the relationship is balance, but it may be achieved with wild swings of the scales on the way, so don't expect a quiet life, though this pair will enjoy a reconciliation after an argument! Material success is probable and, as both like children, a family is likely. Star rating: ***

Taurus meets Virgo

This is a difficult basis for a successful relationship, and yet it often works. Both signs are from the Earth element, so have a common-sense approach to life. They have a mutual understanding, and share many interests. Taurus understands and copes well with Virgo's fussy nature, while Virgo revels in the Bull's tidy and artistic qualities. Both sides are committed to achieving lasting material success. There won't be fireworks, and the match may lack a certain 'spiritual' feel, but as that works both ways it may not be a problem. Star rating: *****

Taurus meets Libra

A happy life is important to both these signs and, as they are both ruled by Venus, they share a common understanding, even though they display themselves so differently. Taurus is quieter than Libra, but can be decisive, and that's what counts. Libra is interested in absolutely everything, an infectious quality when seen through Taurean eyes. The slightly flighty qualities of Libra may lead to jealousy from the Bull. Not an argumentative relationship and one that often works well. There could be many changes of address for this pair. Star rating: ****

Taurus meets Scorpio

Scorpio is deep – very deep – which may be a problem, because Taurus doesn't wear its heart on its sleeve either. It might be difficult for this pair to get together, because neither are naturally inclined to make the first move. Taurus stands in awe of the power and intensity of the Scorpio mind, while the Scorpion is interested in the Bull's affable and friendly qualities, so an enduring relationship could be forged if the couple ever get round to talking. Both are lovers of home and family, which will help to cement a relationship. Star rating: **

Taurus meets Sagittarius

On first impression, Taurus may not like Sagittarius, who may seem brash, and even common, when viewed through the Bull's refined eyes. But there is hope of success because the two signs have so much to offer each other. The Archer is enthralled by the Taurean's natural poise and beauty, while Taurus always needs more basic confidence, which is no problem to Sagittarius who has plenty to spare. Both signs love to travel. There are certain to be ups and downs, but that doesn't prevent an interesting, inspiring and even exciting combination. Star rating: ***

Taurus meets Capricorn

If not quite a match made in heaven, this comes close. Both signs are earthy in nature and that is a promising start. Capricorn is very practical and can make a Taurean's dreams come true. Both are tidy, like to know what is going to happen in a day-to-day sense, and are steady and committed. Taurus loves refinement, which Capricorn accepts and even helps to create. A good prognosis for material success rounds off a relationship that could easily stay the course. The only thing missing is a genuine sense of humour. Star rating: *****

Taurus meets Aquarius

In any relationship of which Aquarius is a part, surprises abound. It is difficult for Taurus to understand the soul-searching, adventurous, changeable Aquarian, but on the positive side, the Bull is adaptable and can respond well to a dose of excitement. Aquarians are kind and react well to the same quality coming back at them. Both are friendly, capable of deep affection and basically quite creative. Unfortunately, though, Taurus simply doesn't know what makes Aquarius tick, which could lead to hidden feelings of isolation. Star rating: **

Taurus meets Pisces

No problem here, unless both parties come from the quieter side of their respective signs. Most of the time Taurus and Pisces would live comfortably together, offering mutual support and deep regard. Taurus can offer the personal qualities that Pisces craves, whilst Pisces understands and copes with the Bull's slightly stubborn qualities. Taurus is likely to travel in Piscean company, so there is a potential for wide-ranging experiences and variety which is essential. There will be some misunderstandings, mainly because Pisces is so deep, but that won't prevent their enduring happiness. Star rating: ***

Taurus meets Aries

This match has been known to work very well. Aries brings dynamism and ambition, while Taurus has the patience to see things through logically. Such complementary views work equally well in a relationship or in an office environment. There is mutual respect, but sometimes a lack of total understanding. The romantic needs of each sign are quite different, but both are still fulfilled. Taurus and Aries can live easily in domestic harmony which is very important but, interestingly, Aries may be the loser in battles of will. Star rating: ***

VENUS: THE PLANET OF LOVE

If you look up at the sky around sunset or sunrise you will often see Venus in close attendance to the Sun. It is arguably one of the most beautiful sights of all and there is little wonder that historically it became associated with the goddess of love. But although Venus does play an important part in the way you view love and in the way others see you romantically, this is only one of the spheres of influence that it enjoys in your overall character.

Venus has a part to play in the more cultured side of your life and has much to do with your appreciation of art, literature, music and general creativity. Even the way you look is responsive to the part of the zodiac that Venus occupied at the start of your life, though this fact is also down to your Sun sign and Ascending sign. If, at the time you were born, Venus occupied one of the more gregarious zodiac signs, you will be more likely to wear your heart on your sleeve, as well as to be more attracted to entertainment, social gatherings and good company. If on the other hand Venus occupied a quiet zodiac sign at the time of your birth, you would tend to be more retiring and less willing to shine in public situations.

It's good to know what part the planet Venus plays in your life, for it can have a great bearing on the way you appear to the rest of the world and since we all have to mix with others, you can learn to make the very best of what Venus has to offer you.

One of the great complications in the past has always been trying to establish exactly what zodiac position Venus enjoyed when you were born, because the planet is notoriously difficult to track. However, we have solved that problem by creating a table that is exclusive to your Sun sign, which you will find on the following page.

Establishing your Venus sign could not be easier. Just look up the year of your birth on the following page and you will see a sign of the zodiac. This was the sign that Venus occupied in the period covered by your sign in that year. If Venus occupied more than one sign during the period, this is indicated by the date on which the sign changed, and the name of the new sign. For instance, if you were born in 1950, Venus was in Pisces until the 5th May, after which time it was in Aries. If you were born before 5th May your Venus sign is Pisces, if you were born on or after 5th May, your Venus sign is Aries. Once you have established the position of Venus at the time of your birth, you can then look in the pages which follow to see how this has a bearing on your life as a whole.

1919 GEMINI / 13.5 CANCER
1920 ARIES / 7.5 TAURUS
1921 TAURUS / 27.4 ARIES
1922 TAURUS / 2.5 GEMINI
1923 PISCES / 27.4 ARIES
1924 GEMINI / 7.5 CANCER
1925 TAURUS / 16.5 GEMINI
1926 PISCES / 6.5 ARIES
1927 GEMINI / 12.5 CANCER
1928 ARIES / 6.5 TAURUS
1929 TAURUS / 24.4 ARIES
1930 TAURUS / 1.5 GEMINI
1931 PISCES / 26.4 ARIES
1932 GEMINI / 8.5 CANCER
1933 TAURUS / 15.5 GEMINI
1934 PISCES / 6.5 ARIES
1935 GEMINI / 12.5 CANCER
1936 ARIES / 6.5 TAURUS
1937 TAURUS / 21.4 ARIES
1938 TAURUS / 1.5 GEMINI
1939 PISCES / 26.4 ARIES
1940 GEMINI / 9.5 CANCER
1941 TAURUS / 14.5 GEMINI
1942 PISCES / 6.5 ARIES
1943 GEMINI / 11.5 CANCER
1944 ARIES / 6.5 TAURUS
1945 ARIES
1946 TAURUS / 30.4 GEMINI
1947 PISCES / 25.4 ARIES
1948 GEMINI / 9.5 CANCER
1949 TAURUS / 14.5 GEMINI
1950 PISCES / 5.5 ARIES
1951 GEMINI / 11.5 CANCER
1952 ARIES / 5.5 TAURUS
1953 ARIES
1954 TAURUS / 29.4 GEMINI
1955 PISCES / 25.4 ARIES
1956 GEMINI / 10.5 CANCER
1957 TAURUS / 13.5 GEMINI
1958 PISCES / 5.5 ARIES
1959 GEMINI / 10.5 CANCER
1960 ARIES / 4.5 TAURUS
1961 ARIES
1962 TAURUS / 28.4 GEMINI
1963 PISCES / 24.4 ARIES
1964 GEMINI / 11.5 CANCER
1965 TAURUS / 13.5 GEMINI
1966 PISCES / 5.5 ARIES
1967 GEMINI / 10.5 CANCER
1968 ARIES / 4.5 TAURUS
1969 ARIES
1970 TAURUS / 27.4 GEMINI
1971 PISCES / 24.4 ARIES
1972 GEMINI / 12.5 CANCER
1973 TAURUS / 12.5 GEMINI
1974 PISCES / 4.5 ARIES
1975 GEMINI / 9.5 CANCER
1976 ARIES / 3.5 TAURUS
1977 ARIES
1978 TAURUS / 27.4 GEMINI
1979 PISCES / 23.4 ARIES
1980 GEMINI / 13.5 CANCER
1981 TAURUS / 12.5 GEMINI
1982 PISCES / 4.5 ARIES
1983 GEMINI / 9.5 CANCER
1984 ARIES / 3.5 TAURUS
1985 ARIES
1986 TAURUS / 26.4 GEMINI
1987 PISCES / 23.4 ARIES
1988 GEMINI / 15.5 CANCER
1989 TAURUS / 11.5 GEMINI
1990 PISCES / 4.5 ARIES
1991 GEMINI / 8.5 CANCER
1992 ARIES / 2.5 TAURUS
1993 ARIES
1994 TAURUS / 26.4 GEMINI
1995 PISCES / 22.4 ARIES
1996 GEMINI / 15.5 CANCER
1997 TAURUS / 11.5 GEMINI
1998 PISCES / 3.5 ARIES
1999 GEMINI / 8.5 CANCER
2000 ARIES / 2.5 TAURUS
2001 ARIES
2002 TAURUS / 26.4 GEMINI
2003 PISCES / 22.4 ARIES
2004 GEMINI / 15.5 CANCER
2005 TAURUS / 11.5 GEMINI
2006 PISCES / 3.5 ARIES
2007 GEMINI / 8.5 CANCER
2008 ARIES / 2.5 TAURUS
2009 ARIES
2010 TAURUS / 26.4 GEMINI
2011 PISCES / 22.4 ARIES
2012 PISCES / 22.4 ARIES
2013 PISCES / 3.5 ARIES
2014 PISCES / 3.5 ARIES
2015 GEMINI / 8.5 CANCER
2016 TAURUS
2017 GEMINI / 15.5 CANCER

VENUS THROUGH THE ZODIAC SIGNS

Venus in Aries

Amongst other things, the position of Venus in Aries indicates a fondness for travel, music and all creative pursuits. Your nature tends to be affectionate and you would try not to create confusion or difficulty for others if it could be avoided. Many people with this planetary position have a great love of the theatre, and mental stimulation is of the greatest importance. Early romantic attachments are common with Venus in Aries, so it is very important to establish a genuine sense of romantic continuity. Early marriage is not recommended, especially if it is based on sympathy. You may give your heart a little too readily on occasions.

Venus in Taurus

You are capable of very deep feelings and your emotions tend to last for a very long time. This makes you a trusting partner and lover, whose constancy is second to none. In life you are precise and careful and always try to do things the right way. Although this means an ordered life, which you are comfortable with, it can also lead you to be rather too fussy for your own good. Despite your pleasant nature, you are very fixed in your opinions and quite able to speak your mind. Others are attracted to you and historical astrologers always quoted this position of Venus as being very fortunate in terms of marriage. However, if you find yourself involved in a failed relationship, it could take you a long time to trust again.

Venus in Gemini

As with all associations related to Gemini, you tend to be quite versatile, anxious for change and intelligent in your dealings with the world at large. You may gain money from more than one source but you are equally good at spending it. There is an inference here that you are a good communicator, via either the written or the spoken word, and you love to be in the company of interesting people. Always on the look-out for culture, you may also be very fond of music, and love to indulge the curious and cultured side of your nature. In romance you tend to have more than one relationship and could find yourself associated with someone who has previously been a friend or even a distant relative.

Venus in Cancer

You often stay close to home because you are very fond of family and enjoy many of your most treasured moments when you are with those you love. Being naturally sympathetic, you will always do anything you can to support those around you, even people you hardly know at all. This charitable side of your nature is your most noticeable trait and is one of the reasons why others are naturally so fond of you. Being receptive and in some cases even psychic, you can see through to the soul of most of those with whom you come into contact. You may not commence too many romantic attachments but when you do give your heart, it tends to be unconditionally.

Venus in Leo

It must become quickly obvious to almost anyone you meet that you are kind, sympathetic and yet determined enough to stand up for anyone or anything that is truly important to you. Bright and sunny, you warm the world with your natural enthusiasm and would rarely do anything to hurt those around you, or at least not intentionally. In romance you are ardent and sincere, though some may find your style just a little overpowering. Gains come through your contacts with other people and this could be especially true with regard to romance, for love and money often come hand in hand for those who were born with Venus in Leo. People claim to understand you, though you are more complex than you seem.

Venus in Virgo

Your nature could well be fairly quiet no matter what your Sun sign might be, though this fact often manifests itself as an inner peace and would not prevent you from being basically sociable. Some delays and even the odd disappointment in love cannot be ruled out with this planetary position, though it's a fact that you will usually find the happiness you look for in the end. Catapulting yourself into romantic entanglements that you know to be rather ill-advised is not sensible, and it would be better to wait before you committed yourself exclusively to any one person. It is the essence of your nature to serve the world at large and through doing so it is possible that you will attract money at some stage in your life.

Venus in Libra

Venus is very comfortable in Libra and bestows upon those people who have this planetary position a particular sort of kindness that is easy to recognise. This is a very good position for all sorts of friendships and also for romantic attachments that usually bring much joy into your life. Few individuals with Venus in Libra would avoid marriage and since you are capable of great depths of love, it is likely that you will find a contented personal life. You like to mix with people of integrity and intelligence but don't take kindly to scruffy surroundings or work that means getting your hands too dirty. Careful speculation, good business dealings and money through marriage all seem fairly likely.

Venus in Scorpio

You are quite open and tend to spend money quite freely, even on those occasions when you don't have very much. Although your intentions are always good, there are times when you get yourself in to the odd scrape and this can be particularly true when it comes to romance, which you may come to late or from a rather unexpected direction. Certainly you have the power to be happy and to make others contented on the way, but you find the odd stumbling block on your journey through life and it could seem that you have to work harder than those around you. As a result of this, you gain a much deeper understanding of the true value of personal happiness than many people ever do, and are likely to achieve true contentment in the end.

Venus in Sagittarius

You are lighthearted, cheerful and always able to see the funny side of any situation. These facts enhance your popularity, which is especially high with members of the opposite sex. You should never have to look too far to find romantic interest in your life, though it is just possible that you might be too willing to commit yourself before you are certain that the person in question is right for you. Part of the problem here extends to other areas of life too. The fact is that you like variety in everything and so can tire of situations that fail to offer it. All the same, if you choose wisely and learn to understand your restless side, then great happiness can be yours.

Venus in Capricorn

The most notable trait that comes from Venus in this position is that it makes you trustworthy and able to take on all sorts of responsibilities in life. People are instinctively fond of you and love you all the more because you are always ready to help those who are in any form of need. Social and business popularity can be yours and there is a magnetic quality to your nature that is particularly attractive in a romantic sense. Anyone who wants a partner for a lover, a spouse and a good friend too would almost certainly look in your direction. Constancy is the hallmark of your nature and unfaithfulness would go right against the grain. You might sometimes be a little too trusting.

Venus in Aquarius

This location of Venus offers a fondness for travel and a desire to try out something new at every possible opportunity. You are extremely easy to get along with and tend to have many friends from varied backgrounds, classes and inclinations. You like to live a distinct sort of life and gain a great deal from moving about, both in a career sense and with regard to your home. It is not out of the question that you could form a romantic attachment to someone who comes from far away or be attracted to a person of a distinctly artistic and original nature. What you cannot stand is jealousy, for you have friends of both sexes and would want to keep things that way.

Venus in Pisces

The first thing people tend to notice about you is your wonderful, warm smile. Being very charitable by nature you will do anything to help others, even if you don't know them well. Much of your life may be spent sorting out situations for other people, but it is very important to feel that you are living for yourself too. In the main, you remain cheerful, and tend to be quite attractive to members of the opposite sex. Where romantic attachments are concerned, you could be drawn to people who are significantly older or younger than yourself or to someone with a unique career or point of view. It might be best for you to avoid marrying whilst you are still very young.

TAURUS:
2016 DIARY PAGES

♉

October

2016

1 SATURDAY *Moon Age Day 1 Moon Sign Libra*

It looks as though this is going to be a good time for stretching your mind and broadening your horizons in some way. Take every opportunity to try something new and don't be held back simply because others don't share your point of view. Avoid family rows by getting out of the house if at all possible.

2 SUNDAY *Moon Age Day 2 Moon Sign Libra*

A great deal of versatility is available to Taurus at the moment, which is nothing especially new to your very capable zodiac sign but comes in handy all the same. Keep a high profile in social situations and let people know that you are available to help at almost any time.

3 MONDAY *Moon Age Day 3 Moon Sign Scorpio*

For the moment you could discover that energy is in short supply. This is not a situation that is going to last very long, so be patient with yourself and with the world at large. Small details probably demand your attention at the moment, which is good because you are excellent at dealing with them.

4 TUESDAY *Moon Age Day 4 Moon Sign Scorpio*

Although you may not be setting the world alight you can make the most of this quiet interlude by taking some time out to think. In one way or another you have learned a great deal in the last few months. Some of it needs to be filed away in your mind for future reference and today offers you that chance.

5 WEDNESDAY *Moon Age Day 5 Moon Sign Scorpio*

Domestic matters now prove particularly demanding and there will be little time to concentrate on work. Even when you are not actually doing things at home the ins and outs of situations will be on your mind. Confidence remains quite high and you won't go short of the right sort of attention.

6 THURSDAY *Moon Age Day 6 Moon Sign Sagittarius*

Current influences should make your life more rewarding, both in a personal and a financial sense. Looking for security around now, you may review your cash resources and could easily discover you are slightly better off than you may have thought. Patience is available when dealing with tricky tasks.

7 FRIDAY *Moon Age Day 7 Moon Sign Sagittarius*

There is a great urge for you to express your opinions today, probably in no uncertain terms. A degree of common sense is necessary because if you are too outspoken you may only cause problems for yourself in the longer-term. All in all it might be best to bite your tongue and to use some diplomacy.

8 SATURDAY *Moon Age Day 8 Moon Sign Capricorn*

Large social groups can be inspirational today, more so than would normally be the case for your zodiac sign. Something new, either at work or at home, probably isn't working as well as you had hoped. If this is the case, try to use it in some novel way, or assess your own competence.

9 SUNDAY *Moon Age Day 9 Moon Sign Capricorn*

Social matters are now likely to be uppermost in your mind. Take advantage of what the day has to offer by keeping in the public eye. You are being watched at present and it appears that you can impress others very easily indeed. Avoid getting into pointless rows with people who don't count at all.

10 MONDAY *Moon Age Day 10 Moon Sign Capricorn*

This is a period when most matters associated with your career seem to be on a roll. Make the most of social trends today, particularly by contacting people you haven't seen for some time. Jobs you don't care for should be tackled early and then you can move on to more pleasurable matters.

11 TUESDAY *Moon Age Day 11 Moon Sign Aquarius*

This is another go-ahead period when it comes to contacting others. Generally speaking you are now keen to spend time with people who have a very happy-go-lucky view of life and you won't have much truck with really miserable types. Keep a sense of proportion regarding matters of the heart.

12 WEDNESDAY *Moon Age Day 12 Moon Sign Aquarius*

Ready yourself for new social contacts and make the best of what they have to offer when they turn up. Get out and about today because staying within your own four walls could prove to be rather tedious. Concentrate on solving the problems of family members, some of which don't look too complicated from your perspective.

13 THURSDAY *Moon Age Day 13 Moon Sign Pisces*

Disagreements with others are more or less inevitable at some stage today. Keep them to a minimum if you can because they aren't much use and merely serve to disrupt your routines. Confidence to do the right thing in social settings means that you progress rapidly in the eyes and views of others.

14 FRIDAY *Moon Age Day 14 Moon Sign Pisces*

When it comes to exchanging ideas with others you are second to none right now. Talk as much as you can, though to people who are in the know. Idle chit-chat, though interesting enough in its own way, doesn't have too much to offer for now. Creative potential appears to be especially good. Perhaps try painting a picture?

15 SATURDAY *Moon Age Day 15 Moon Sign Aries*

The more the merrier seems to be your personal adage at the moment. Saturday finds you involved with others, and maybe taking the chance to fit in a shopping trip. If you are buying things for your home do shop around. There is still enough good luck present to assure you of some sort of bargain.

16 SUNDAY *Moon Age Day 16 Moon Sign Aries*

New information is likely to put you fully in the picture today and allows you to make progress in many different areas of your life. However, this progress is only potential and much depends on your own efforts. This is not a time to be a shrinking violet and you do need to act decisively on occasion.

17 MONDAY *Moon Age Day 17 Moon Sign Taurus*

With the lunar high comes a certainty in your mind that you are going in the right direction generally speaking. Take advantage of every opportunity to make a good impression and be prepared to push your luck as much as you can. There is room for variation in your schedule today, which the position of the Moon supports.

18 TUESDAY *Moon Age Day 18 Moon Sign Taurus*

See what Lady Luck can do for you today by putting yourself in her path. This can be a quite glorious time for some Taureans, particularly if you have realised that life is going your way more than you expected. With everything to play for in terms of love, exactly the right words come into your mind now.

19 WEDNESDAY *Moon Age Day 19 Moon Sign Gemini*

There could be some slight difficulties at work today. Maybe you are not communicating as well with others as would normally be the case. You need to exhibit some patience in your dealings with colleagues, a few of whom could appear to be playing rather silly games. Socially, life should be secure enough.

20 THURSDAY *Moon Age Day 20 Moon Sign Gemini*

There is good potential for attracting new people into your life, either in the workplace or socially. This stage of the working week is quite likely to bring you into contact with types who can be of specific use to you practically, though by the evening you will be opting for fun.

21 FRIDAY *Moon Age Day 21 Moon Sign Cancer*

Your judgement is very good and you can afford to trust your own conclusions in most matters. Relationships may offer the best way forward today, as would a shopping excursion or perhaps a social event planned at the last minute. Make the most of new friendships that could easily come along now.

22 SATURDAY *Moon Age Day 22 Moon Sign Cancer*

A friend or social contact is likely to be trying your patience now. It would be good to spread your influence socially and there is certainly no need to fall out with anyone. Social trends remain generally good but it's likely that you will be turning more and more to family members in order to fill your quiet hours at present.

23 SUNDAY *Moon Age Day 23 Moon Sign Leo*

You should have little or no trouble staying in the good books of others today. Popularity remains high and it appears that you know exactly what to say in order to get the right sort of reaction from others. Campaigns that you have embarked upon need dealing with very carefully. Don't rush your fences.

24 MONDAY *Moon Age Day 24 Moon Sign Leo*

This could be a very enthusiastic sort of day for many sons and daughters of Taurus. Although you won't always know how to proceed under every given circumstance, you are very good at thinking on your feet. Remove any doubt in the mind of a friend regarding your keenness for specific new projects.

25 TUESDAY *Moon Age Day 25 Moon Sign Leo*

Today's planetary trends bring a potentially busy time and a period when you can gain from the viewpoints of friends and colleagues alike. At present you are able to bring out the best in others, many of whom will want to assist you for no reason other than their affection for your bright and sunny nature.

26 WEDNESDAY *Moon Age Day 26 Moon Sign Virgo*

Socially speaking you are now likely to be drawn to the new and unusual in life. Not that there is much time to take notice today. Life is hectic, probably because of the needs that others have of you. There are moments when rules and regulations could so easily get on your nerves if you can't find ways to ignore them.

27 THURSDAY *Moon Age Day 27 Moon Sign Virgo*

Along comes a more pleasurable period socially than may have been the case for the last couple of days. In conversation you now show yourself to be frank, free and possibly even a little outspoken. There are gains to be made in the area of friendship and good trends pointing towards a more progressive phase in personal attachments.

28 FRIDAY *Moon Age Day 28 Moon Sign Libra*

Things definitely appear to go better in pairs today. This is as true in a practical sense as it is personally. It will undoubtedly be your intention to finish the working week with a flourish. By the evening it should become apparent that you are running out of steam. The lunar low is not too far away and that might mean getting some rest.

29 SATURDAY *Moon Age Day 29 Moon Sign Libra*

Work matters offer continued scope for advancement, though of course this might be theoretical rather than practical on a Saturday. In practical matters you show how capable you can be and can easily turn heads in close, one-to-one situations. Keep an eye on money because it might be multiplying somehow.

30 SUNDAY *Moon Age Day 0 Moon Sign Libra*

Though group and co-operative ventures tend to go smoothly enough today it is in the direction of personal relationships that your mind turns. Mixing freely with your friends, you could discover that one or two of them hold a key that can open some very interesting doors for you.

31 MONDAY *Moon Age Day 1 Moon Sign Scorpio*

There are some curious situations around at the moment and since you wish to resolve them a little detective work may be in order. Make certain that you are not wasting time on needless distractions because there is enough to do now without going down pointless roads. Scrutinise any documents that need signing carefully.

November

2016

1 TUESDAY *Moon Age Day 2 Moon Sign Scorpio*

You can't avoid feeling that life is turning against you in some way, though of course this isn't the case and you are simply coming up against the lunar low. Take time out and look at matters with a greater degree of concentration. All Taurus people need to meditate now and again and this is as good a time as any to do it.

2 WEDNESDAY *Moon Age Day 3 Moon Sign Sagittarius*

Clever communication is called for at the moment and that is what you are able to supply. Planetary trends now begin to work in your favour once more, offering you a silver tongue at the time you need it the most. Today has much to offer and particularly so if you are willing to move with changing times.

3 THURSDAY *Moon Age Day 4 Moon Sign Sagittarius*

Along comes a period of swifter progress. If you hurry right now you can steal a march on someone who has been irritating you for a while, though without doing them any direct harm. What matters at present is convincing yourself that you are more capable than you previously thought.

4 FRIDAY *Moon Age Day 5 Moon Sign Sagittarius*

It appears that you can get a great deal from a complete change of scene now, even though that might be somewhat difficult to organise. Generally speaking you like to keep things the same but that can lead to a degree of stagnation. Overturn the bounds of the credible and prove what a fun-loving soul you are at the same time.

5 SATURDAY *Moon Age Day 6 Moon Sign Capricorn*

It is now easy for you to shine in social and family matters, during a period that is very well accented in the area of close personal attachments. Where there has been a little discord, now you find reconciliation and warmth. It may not be your own attitude that has changed at all but rather the ideas and opinions of others.

6 SUNDAY *Moon Age Day 7 Moon Sign Capricorn*

Matters of the heart could seem, for the moment, to be somewhat constrictive. It's true that the recent past may not have been the easiest you have ever lived through in this regard, but the situation will improve markedly in the days ahead. Use today in a fairly flippant way and don't try to get ahead too much.

7 MONDAY *Moon Age Day 8 Moon Sign Aquarius*

Some care is necessary at the start of this week when it comes to expressing your ego to the world at large. Split your time between the needs of your home life and the requirements of the practical world. Establish a better contact with those who may have alienated themselves from you of late.

8 TUESDAY *Moon Age Day 9 Moon Sign Aquarius*

There is a strong social boost to the day, together with new incentives that might look particularly exciting. Think about all outings to places of entertainment and when it comes to having a good time in the company of pals, don't hold back. Almost everyone wants to be your friend now.

9 WEDNESDAY *Moon Age Day 10 Moon Sign Pisces*

Although personal relationships might be somewhat in the doldrums today, you take your joys where you can find them. For now that means friendship and the support specific individuals are offering. In a practical sense it would be best not to take anything for granted, particularly at work.

10 THURSDAY *Moon Age Day 11 Moon Sign Pisces*

A specific scheme that you have been hatching recently might be found to contain certain glitches. It would be a shame to come so far and then to abandon something that might work very well. Instead, see what you can do in order to make a few running repairs. Friendship is still very important.

11 FRIDAY *Moon Age Day 12 Moon Sign Pisces*

There is much to be said for staying out there in the social world at present, particularly because your personal life may not be offering everything you would wish. Keep up your efforts to achieve a coup at work, but leave some time to enjoy yourself, especially with the weekend in view.

12 SATURDAY *Moon Age Day 13 Moon Sign Aries*

Existing deep attachments might be the least inspiring aspect of your life right now. The answer is simple. Keep your connection to others light, simple and free from any form of aggravation. As long as you are smiling the world will offer you its own grin. There's a danger you are taking yourself too seriously.

13 SUNDAY *Moon Age Day 14 Moon Sign Aries*

Focusing on the small details right now gives you what you need to get in front of the pack. Although you may not be rushing ahead like some people, you are being careful and that is what counts. Whilst others have to repeat procedures time and again, you are getting them right first time round.

14 MONDAY *Moon Age Day 15 Moon Sign Taurus*

Today is likely to be very successful from a personal point of view. It is clear that you relish the company of interesting and witty people and that you can get ahead in ways you haven't been expecting. For all this you can thank the lunar high, but also your own ingenuity and common sense.

15 TUESDAY *Moon Age Day 16 Moon Sign Taurus*

A word in the right ear can work virtual miracles at present. Give yourself fully to all that the day has to offer, and particularly so after a period that really hasn't worked out quite the way you would have wished. Making progress in matters of the heart and really enjoying yourself are what today is about.

16 WEDNESDAY *Moon Age Day 17 Moon Sign Gemini*

Your social life might be something of a letdown at the moment. If so, you probably are not dealing with specific people in the right way. Certainly you should not allow yourself to be held back by negative attitudes. Leave alone those individuals who insist on taking a pessimistic approach to life.

17 THURSDAY *Moon Age Day 18 Moon Sign Gemini*

Along comes a day for positive social relations and one that finds you distinctly more 'up front' than appears to have been the case recently. Sort out any routines early in the day and don't be afraid to have some fun. People may notice your tendency to tease others at present, but this is hardly likely to be a stumbling block.

18 FRIDAY *Moon Age Day 19 Moon Sign Cancer*

A get-up-and-go mood will be apparent to everyone you meet. Of course this won't be much help if you stay locked in your own home all day. It's important to 'contribute' in every sense of the word today. It shouldn't be too difficult to find individuals who will be happy to help you enjoy yourself.

19 SATURDAY *Moon Age Day 20 Moon Sign Cancer*

You will probably choose actively to be on the move during the course of your daily affairs for the moment. Staying in one place and doing exactly what is expected of you is hardly likely to be much fun and there is so much scope for having a good time it seems rather pointless to restrict yourself unduly.

20 SUNDAY *Moon Age Day 21 Moon Sign Leo*

If your domestic life threatens to get in the way of personal freedom this Sunday it will be necessary to find some sort of solution. The balance of life is extremely important this weekend, so don't allow yourself to be browbeaten into doing things at home that go against the grain. Change and diversity are important.

21 MONDAY *Moon Age Day 22 Moon Sign Leo*

A new working week brings a slightly more cautious approach than usual. This is particularly noticeable in a financial sense. Maybe you are saving your money for a rainy day or perhaps you feel that someone doesn't have your best material interests at heart. Whatever the reason you don't want to spend freely at present.

22 TUESDAY *Moon Age Day 23 Moon Sign Virgo*

Your persuasive powers over others are pretty strong today, so if there is anything you really want, now is the time to go out and ask for it. It won't be as simple as that of course, though nobody you care for will refuse reasonable requests. Socially speaking you seem to be reaching a high and may be planning well ahead.

23 WEDNESDAY *Moon Age Day 24 Moon Sign Virgo*

Career matters that lack direction should be dealt with firmly and immediately right now. Don't let things stew in your life generally and do be willing to take the sort of decisions that you know to be sensible. Attitudes towards loved ones vary, especially if some of them are being deliberately awkward.

24 THURSDAY *Moon Age Day 25 Moon Sign Libra*

Partnerships are likely to offer a comfortable aspect to life as the working week moves onward. For some of you this will be a career matter, though in the vast majority of cases it is personal attachments that are to the fore. A Thursday of fun is not beyond your grasp, even if things are slowing down somewhat at present.

25 FRIDAY *Moon Age Day 26 Moon Sign Libra*

There are some tests around when it comes to keeping your life on an even keel. Interest and imagination come along in great measure, allowing you to feel that you are positively involved in a number of situations that have probably been closed to you in the past. Creative potential is good now and remains so for some time.

26 SATURDAY *Moon Age Day 27 Moon Sign Libra*

Relationships are almost certain to be happy and contented right now. Whether the people you deal with have been known to you for years, or have just entered your life, you know exactly how to get on well with them. In working situations it is plain that you can rely on colleagues to a high degree now.

27 SUNDAY *Moon Age Day 28 Moon Sign Scorpio*

This is hardly the most dynamic part of the month for Taurus but how this has a bearing on your life really depends on the way you choose to respond to these trends. Keep up your efforts to improve your life generally and don't allow yourself to be thwarted by situations that you can deal with relatively easily.

28 MONDAY *Moon Age Day 29 Moon Sign Scorpio*

Maybe you should be willing to allow those closest to you to make some of the decisions at present. The fact is that the lunar low can take the wind out of your sails and more or less demands a reasonably quiet sort of period. This won't bother you unduly after such a busy time in the recent past.

29 TUESDAY *Moon Age Day 0 Moon Sign Sagittarius*

A much more decisive edge now becomes apparent as far as your general nature is concerned. You have many ways and means of achieving your objectives today and even a little subterfuge isn't out of the question. Where affairs of the heart are concerned you seem willing to be swayed by reason.

30 WEDNESDAY *Moon Age Day 1 Moon Sign Sagittarius*

This is likely to be a good day for getting on with work commitments. Almost anyone you know will make themselves useful to you at this time and there is no shame whatsoever in being willing to ask for help. On the contrary, doing so is highly likely to get you noticed.

December

2016

1 THURSDAY *Moon Age Day 2 Moon Sign Sagittarius*

It's the first day of December and also time to keep your eyes open. There are some gains to be made, especially in terms of finance. Things are looking good in the material world for Taurus and it seems that you really have your wits about you now. Discussions at this time can reveal some interesting facts.

2 FRIDAY *Moon Age Day 3 Moon Sign Capricorn*

All things domestic capture your imagination and also demand your time. Confidence is still present when you need it the most and you should be finding plenty to keep you occupied. Don't be surprised if your nearest and dearest begin to complain that you are not doing enough planning for Christmas.

3 SATURDAY *Moon Age Day 4 Moon Sign Capricorn*

Pursuits that allow your imagination to run free are the ones that will appeal to you the most today. There is plenty of variety about in life and you want to make the most of it. Concentrate on the practical in life and you will continue to benefit from the hard work you have put in recently.

4 SUNDAY *Moon Age Day 5 Moon Sign Aquarius*

Sunday should find you happy to be the centre of attention. True, you are going to be up against competition and some people at least won't allow you to get all your own way now. Creative potential is good, so it is possible that you will use at least part of today doing jobs in and around your home.

5 MONDAY *Moon Age Day 6 Moon Sign Aquarius*

Your inquisitive qualities are much sharpened at the beginning of this week and it is clear that you want to know how the world works. There is a good deal of trivia about too, which you could well do without. Striking the right sort of balance between fulfilling responsibilities and yet pleasing yourself could be difficult.

6 TUESDAY *Moon Age Day 7 Moon Sign Aquarius*

Getting your own way can be somewhat difficult now but things will change very quickly. Something you were looking forward to might let you down and people can be appear quite unreliable too. Take life one step at a time, refuse to rush your fences and simply exhibit that genuine Taurean patience.

7 WEDNESDAY *Moon Age Day 8 Moon Sign Pisces*

A good day for asking questions and for garnering new information about life on all levels. Don't be fooled into thinking that you are getting a bargain, when you know in your heart that you are being conned. Actually it would be very difficult for anyone to pull the wool over your eyes right now.

8 THURSDAY *Moon Age Day 9 Moon Sign Pisces*

Getting stuck with mundane routines won't appeal to you very much at all now. On the contrary you are more likely to be busy in a practical sense and away from home for at least some of the time. People are relying heavily on you, though some of them are willing to offer you a great deal in return.

9 FRIDAY *Moon Age Day 10 Moon Sign Aries*

Now that the Moon is in your solar twelfth house it is quite possible that you will deliberately choose to take a low profile. Taurus is not the noisiest sign of the zodiac in any case but right now you will be quite satisfied with your own company. Pushing ahead in terms of work does seem to be quite possible.

10 SATURDAY *Moon Age Day 11 Moon Sign Aries*

This seems to be your month when it comes to love and romance. Young or young-at-heart Taurus types can expect present attachments to firm up, or new ones to raise their heads at any time now. More secure and settled individuals should register a greater degree of personal support and encouragement.

11 SUNDAY *Moon Age Day 12 Moon Sign Taurus*

This is the best part of the month for fresh starts and for getting ahead with unfinished work. Everything goes with a swing now and you can impress people as easily as falling off a log. Popularity ought to be high and because you are not in the mood for work you will certainly show others that you know how to have a good time.

12 MONDAY *Moon Age Day 13 Moon Sign Taurus*

It is possible that you will now feel that not enough is happening in your vicinity. If this does turn out to be the case you need to put in that extra bit of effort that can make all the difference later on. There are slightly quieter times at hand, at least there could be unless you act decisively today.

13 TUESDAY *Moon Age Day 14 Moon Sign Gemini*

If you are involved in discussions today it is possible that you will have to guard your tongue. Speaking out of turn now could bring problems further down the line. The right sort of circumstances to allow material progress may not be present just for the moment though they aren't long in turning up.

14 WEDNESDAY *Moon Age Day 15 Moon Sign Gemini*

There is some conflict arising between what you know you should be doing for others and yet those things that are specifically important to you. Although you are more than capable of standing up for yourself at present, it might not be a bad idea to rely on friends who are more than willing to lend a hand.

15 THURSDAY *Moon Age Day 16 Moon Sign Cancer*

The sort of personal strengths that can have a great bearing on your life might appear to be missing at the moment but this clearly isn't the case. True you are being quite careful, but that's not too strange for Taurus. Confidence to do the right thing remains basically strong, even if there is a little hesitance.

16 FRIDAY *Moon Age Day 17 Moon Sign Cancer*

Since you need to express yourself fully now there's a chance you will be so busy talking that you will overlook a few fairly important details. This isn't like you as a rule but then nobody is perfect! What might really get your goat at the moment are rules and regulations for which you can see no real justification.

17 SATURDAY *Moon Age Day 18 Moon Sign Leo*

Mercury races to your aid when it comes to boosting intellectual interests of all kinds. Others may describe you as ingenious right now which is gratifying, even if you don't necessarily believe it. It shouldn't be hard to sort out the genuine compliments from those comments that are merely intended to curry favour.

18 SUNDAY *Moon Age Day 19 Moon Sign Leo*

New input comes from any number of different directions. Listen to what is being said in your vicinity because it's quite possible that you can learn something useful. Friends should be extra supportive, but that's only because you have put yourself out to help them so many times in the past.

19 MONDAY *Moon Age Day 20 Moon Sign Virgo*

Withdrawing into your own little cocoon could appear very comfortable today. Since it isn't really that long to Christmas it might be sensible to conserve your energy somewhat. The sort of things that will most probably interest you at the moment would include spending time with your partner or family members.

20 TUESDAY ☿ *Moon Age Day 21 Moon Sign Virgo*

Socially speaking you ought to be fairly impressive now. There are plenty of people around on whom you can try out your present skills and since most of them appear to care for you the job should be easy. What might be somewhat more of a problem now is coming to terms with potential changes at work.

21 WEDNESDAY ☿ *Moon Age Day 22 Moon Sign Virgo*

Along comes a time for capitalising on all recent advances at work. It really is time to strike while the iron is hot and to do things before Christmas actually arrives. In a family sense not everyone is likely to be equally helpful and many of the everyday responsibilities appear to be falling on you.

22 THURSDAY ☿ *Moon Age Day 23 Moon Sign Libra*

You may think that you are in the right about most issues today. Of course this could be true, but this attitude won't help much in a moment-by-moment sense. There are occasions when it would be sensible to give others the benefit of the doubt. Close ties work better than friendships or working relationships right now.

23 FRIDAY ☿ *Moon Age Day 24 Moon Sign Libra*

Now that the Sun has entered your solar ninth house, the 'real you' makes a timely appearance. Settling down within yourself, the way you view the world at large is now more realistic and you should find plenty to enjoy. There are gains to be made from going with the flow socially, even if this means doing something that you hadn't planned in advance.

24 SATURDAY ☿ *Moon Age Day 25 Moon Sign Scorpio*

December's lunar low brings a warning not to take anything for granted. Check and double-check all details and stay away from needless speculation. Go for gold in sporting activities, but not unless you know for sure that you are not putting yourself into any danger. Exercise caution in all matters.

25 SUNDAY ☿ *Moon Age Day 26 Moon Sign Scorpio*

Although Christmas coincides with the arrival of the lunar low, as far as you are concerned it is unlikely to be spoiled or diminished. What it might mean is that you feel more secure at home and in the bosom of your family but that is what Christmas is supposed to be about after all.

26 MONDAY ☿ *Moon Age Day 27 Moon Sign Scorpio*

In terms of personal relationships you are now heading for a fairly uncertain period. Perhaps you are simply not in the right frame of mind to elicit the right sort of responses. On the other hand it might be that those around you seem determined to be awkward. It would be sensible not to allow arguments to ensue.

27 TUESDAY ☿ *Moon Age Day 28 Moon Sign Sagittarius*

Social developments are now positively highlighted, allowing you to make the most of the time between now and the new year. Taurus becomes a genuine party animal and you know how to help others to have a good time too. The everyday responsibilities of life are now shelved.

28 WEDNESDAY ☿ *Moon Age Day 29 Moon Sign Sagittarius*

Any number of speculative matters could turn your way right now and you can afford to take the odd chance in life. As the day wears on it is likely that you will be running out of steam physically, though it's clear that your mind is working well and that you are in a position of offer some sound advice.

29 THURSDAY ☿ *Moon Age Day 0 Moon Sign Capricorn*

Major duties and obligations might well get in the way of your need to spread yourself around. Nevertheless this is a time when priority should be given to those tasks you know to be of supreme importance. Ultimately, responsibility is the keyword for all people born under the sign of Taurus.

30 FRIDAY ☿ *Moon Age Day 1 Moon Sign Capricorn*

Your approach to certain emotional matters might not be as positive as you had first intended. If this turns out to be the case you will simply have to try again. Realising that you are capable of getting it wrong is the first step on an important inward journey. Social trends still look good and enjoyment is on the cards.

31 SATURDAY ☿ *Moon Age Day 2 Moon Sign Capricorn*

This is a real 'off with the old and on with the new' end to the year. Overturning conventions isn't your thing as a rule but you are well able to do it now. If necessary, spend some time on a job you really don't want to undertake. You are flexible and adaptable and you will breeze through the celebrations.

TAURUS:
2017 DIARY PAGES

TAURUS: YOUR YEAR IN BRIEF

As the year begins you should find yourself on good form and fairly anxious to get on with projects left over from last year. There are gains to be made during January and February by putting yourself forward and as a result of good financial planning. The winter weather may be something of a trial and you won't have quite the level of energy you would wish but you will be positive and optimistic.

The early spring brings a desire to test yourself and there should be plenty of opportunities to do so. March and April will bring better organisational skills and a feeling that your efforts are now more appreciated. In terms of your courage and stamina you should now be up for anything and you won't easily give in when you know that the path you are choosing is the right one.

During the early summer you will be quite at home wherever you happen to be. May and June bring the chance to ring the changes and travel. You are likely to get on well with people who haven't figured in your life before and you may even put right a few mistakes from the past. Old wounds are healed and relationships across the board seem to be working out especially well for you.

The high summer and July and August should bring you closer to some of your principle desires. There are gains to be made in terms of your financial standing and you may be in the market for a major alteration at work. Taureans who have been thinking about a change of house are likely to embark upon such an adventure, and you may also be more inclined to travel long distances. This is also a time to greet people you haven't seen for ages.

As the year moves on, September and October bring you to the brink of your heart's desire and offer a sense of security. You may not be moving about quite as much but then most of your really good times will be at home or with close friends. You could increase your income at this time and should be on fine form socially and romantically. A new and important friendship is likely to start during this period.

The last two months of the year, November and December, will find you up to speed and more than anxious to get whatever you can from life. You should be at your very best around the Christmas period and will be anxious to join in the fun as only you can. Newer and better romantic prospects are in store for some as the year closes. At the very end of December you might discover something about yourself that you never previously suspected and the discovery should be fascinating.

♉

January

2017

1 SUNDAY ☿ *Moon Age Day 4 Moon Sign Aquarius*

Practical matters could be taking up at least some of your time today, even though the memory of last night's celebration could be etched on your mind – and maybe your stomach! Still, it's a new year and that means getting on with new things as far as Taurus is concerned. You will soon be back into your usual swing.

2 MONDAY ☿ *Moon Age Day 5 Moon Sign Aquarius*

Some of your relationships with others could be slightly too tense right now and that means you have to tread especially carefully if you don't want to cause any offence. Maybe you simply don't have the level of tact that is really necessary if you want to get your own way and if this is the case you should wait to make your approach later.

3 TUESDAY ☿ *Moon Age Day 6 Moon Sign Pisces*

You need to keep up quite a high profile today if you are not to be overlooked in favour of someone else. The trouble is that Taurus is not always the noisiest or most immediately obvious person, so a little extra effort may be required. It's time to wear your brightest clothes or do something slightly outrageous.

4 WEDNESDAY ☿ *Moon Age Day 7 Moon Sign Pisces*

At work, it is possible that someone will put you firmly in the picture today and as a result you could be getting on much better. People will notice you much more today and you are now in the best possible position to put your point of view forward in a very confident way. Socially speaking, you may be slightly more anonymous.

5 THURSDAY ☿ *Moon Age Day 8 Moon Sign Aries*

Your general everyday encounters today should have a very fulfilling quality about them and it is clear that you are feeling fairly optimistic now. You can bring romantic issues to a peak and may also find that you have an unexpected admirer. It is also possible that an acquaintance could become much more.

6 FRIDAY ☿ *Moon Age Day 9 Moon Sign Aries*

Do your best to seek out stimulating experiences with your friends. This enables you to bring out the best in yourself and also others and you certainly should not go short of attention under present planetary trends. It may be necessary to get to grips with a personal issue later in the day, but a little conversation should settle things nicely.

7 SATURDAY ☿ *Moon Age Day 10 Moon Sign Taurus*

The Moon now moves into your own zodiac sign of Taurus, bringing that part of the month known as the lunar high. There is likely to be a sudden and even unexpected burst of energy on your part and it would be hard to avoid the conclusion that Lady Luck is also on your side. Put in your best effort now for maximum results.

8 SUNDAY *Moon Age Day 11 Moon Sign Taurus*

Practical affairs become easier to control, though it is also clear that with the Moon in Taurus you will want to do everything you can to have fun. This is likely to be a Sunday during which you would be happy to be out and about with your friends and when it comes to painting the town red, you will have the biggest brush of all.

9 MONDAY *Moon Age Day 12 Moon Sign Gemini*

You are likely to be on a real winner in terms of your social life – mainly because you are so popular with others. It seems as though you are never short of a good idea for having fun and you will also revel in the chance to travel just at the moment. Don't be too quick to take command in settings you neither understand nor like.

10 TUESDAY *Moon Age Day 13 Moon Sign Gemini*

Your challenge today may be to keep on top of things in a professional sense. Although it is possible that some small irritations could occur, you will be especially good at thinking on your feet, so much so that you can turn a disadvantage around completely and impress more than a few people on the way.

11 WEDNESDAY *Moon Age Day 14 Moon Sign Cancer*

Your skill at getting your own way continues apace, and because you are also quite intuitive at the moment you may have a good idea of the way others are likely to behave. This gives you a definite edge and an ability to judge what moves to make in order to feather your nest both now and later.

12 THURSDAY *Moon Age Day 15 Moon Sign Cancer*

This would be one of the best times of the month for getting involved in a new partnership of some kind. You co-operate well with others and don't get too hung up on details or specifics right now. It should certainly be much easier than usual to give someone the benefit of the doubt. Energy levels will be average.

13 FRIDAY *Moon Age Day 16 Moon Sign Cancer*

Keep your ears open today because there are things being said in your vicinity that are going to be of tremendous importance to you. Even the most casual of conversations could contain clues as to how you can get on better in some way and at the very least the things you hear will keep you suitably entertained during Friday.

14 SATURDAY *Moon Age Day 17 Moon Sign Leo*

You could end up firmly in the limelight this weekend, if only because you are so attractive to certain other people at the moment. Attitude is now extremely important when it comes to getting your own way. A knowing smile, a kind word and a few distinctly charitable actions are all you need to get on extremely well.

15 SUNDAY *Moon Age Day 18 Moon Sign Leo*

As you get down to brass tacks today it becomes quite obvious that you are in the market to make money. This might not sit comfortably with anyone who thinks they have more right to the cash than you do, and the result may be some sort of competition but you are so determined and stubborn you are unlikely to lose.

16 MONDAY *Moon Age Day 19 Moon Sign Virgo*

Culture and the possibility of travel interest you at the moment. You should be feeling on top form and won't be comfortable standing in the shadows. Although Taurus can sometimes be hesitant or shy, this isn't the impression you are giving to the world at large throughout the remainder of this week.

17 TUESDAY *Moon Age Day 20 Moon Sign Virgo*

Take full advantage of your abilities when it comes to communicating. This is likely to be a very social sort of period and you are almost certain to make a good impression on people who can be useful to you in one way or another. In some tasks it may be necessary to go back to basics and to start again if you have to.

18 WEDNESDAY *Moon Age Day 21 Moon Sign Libra*

Your thought processes are very sharp at this stage of the week and you won't have to try very hard in order to get ahead. People you don't see frequently are likely to return to your life and could bring with them exciting news that might lead to travel for you. Long-term plans are easily dealt with now.

19 THURSDAY *Moon Age Day 22 Moon Sign Libra*

Don't hide your light under a bushel at this time. If there is something you know, which you feel others should know, you should be willing to speak out, no matter what company you happen to be in. Active and enterprising, you have what it takes to get ahead professionally and socially. Money matters are variable but improving.

20 FRIDAY *Moon Age Day 23 Moon Sign Scorpio*

The Moon now enters the sign of Scorpio, your opposite zodiac sign, which brings that part of the month known as the lunar low. The result is that you have less energy and need more time to yourself than might sometimes be the case. Don't take on anything too strenuous now or over the weekend and find ways to relax.

21 SATURDAY *Moon Age Day 24 Moon Sign Scorpio*

You still will not be firing on all cylinders and might need to rely on others in order to get something important done. You might feel that not everyone has your best interests at heart, but your sense of perspective is affected by your overall mood and it is possible that you are making more out of certain situations than they really deserve.

22 SUNDAY *Moon Age Day 25 Moon Sign Scorpio*

You are a person who relishes being on the move and exploring new territory and under present trends that is exactly what you will be doing. You might want to wrap up against the winter weather because you were born under a spring zodiac sign, but you won't be lacking in emotional warmth.

23 MONDAY *Moon Age Day 26 Moon Sign Sagittarius*

Trends suggest that you may experience some social developments today. Your ruling planet, Venus, proves to be especially helpful to you around this time. You should be able to find the right words to sweep someone you love off their feet and you won't stick fast when it comes to making important gestures. There is little wonder everyone loves you.

24 TUESDAY *Moon Age Day 27 Moon Sign Sagittarius*

You may find this is one of the better days of the month to prepare for tasks ahead. Keep an eye on the clock because there is much to be done and only you to do it. Of course you could turn some jobs over to others but the way you are feeling at the moment it is unlikely that they would perform to your exacting standards.

25 WEDNESDAY *Moon Age Day 28 Moon Sign Capricorn*

You are in the middle of an excellent time for self-promotion and this goes far beyond professional matters. In romance, friendships or any area of life you can give people a run for their money. Be open to new ideas because some of the advantages that may come along today are not even in your mind when you get out of bed.

26 THURSDAY *Moon Age Day 29 Moon Sign Capricorn*

You reap all the benefits of teamwork and co-operation – whether in a professional or a social sense. Family members can be somewhat trying at present, mainly because what they want for their own lives is not what you would wish on their behalf. A compromise or two will be called for and it's up to you to start the ball rolling.

27 FRIDAY *Moon Age Day 0 Moon Sign Capricorn*

You continue to enjoy sharing interesting ideas and swapping stories with anyone who is willing to listen. Someone who was previously a casual acquaintance may become one of your closest friends very soon and this could coincide with a desire to move in new circles. New interests are a must around this time.

28 SATURDAY *Moon Age Day 1 Moon Sign Aquarius*

Turn towards creative and imaginative ideas for the weekend. If the day is your own and you are not working you can afford to 'waste' a little time today. In the end nothing is wasted because you can turn leisure and pleasure to your distinct advantage. Keep abreast of current affairs and read the local paper.

29 SUNDAY *Moon Age Day 2 Moon Sign Aquarius*

Make the most of harmonious trends to improve your social life. Trends suggest that people around you will want to be on your side and will help you get on in life. You tend to respond in kind, offering as many favours as you can. Some jobs might seem endless but just plough on in your own sweet way.

30 MONDAY *Moon Age Day 3 Moon Sign Pisces*

Expect to glean some new information today. Ingenious and imaginative, you will be right at the front of the queue when it comes to making the most of any situation. If you act on impulse socially, you may create some unexpectedly good times.

31 TUESDAY *Moon Age Day 4 Moon Sign Pisces*

Discipline yourself to finish difficult or tedious tasks that may be weighing on your mind, and once these are done, you can turn to more enjoyable matters with a gratifying sense of achievement. An early start to the day would be good – that way you will feel pleased with all you have managed to achieve.

February 2017

1 WEDNESDAY *Moon Age Day 5 Moon Sign Aries*

Work and professional issues generally should work out well for you today and there is every reason to think that you will find the necessary concentration you need easy to generate. Once responsibilities are out of the way there is a quieter side within your nature that could see you isolating yourself a little.

2 THURSDAY *Moon Age Day 6 Moon Sign Aries*

You have some sound practical ideas to follow at present, and should not be feeling the need to make a fuss about them. You simply get on and see things through to their logical conclusions – at least logical as far as you are concerned. It might be necessary to explain your strategies to others.

3 FRIDAY *Moon Age Day 7 Moon Sign Aries*

Make this a stimulating day and one during which you are not worried about furthering your own ambitions. You can't expect to get on well with everyone and might find that you are particularly frustrated with those people who are inclined to criticise but not motivated to make improvements.

4 SATURDAY *Moon Age Day 8 Moon Sign Taurus*

Most personal pursuits are now likely to be positively highlighted and there isn't much doubt that you will be anxious to get ahead. In almost every way your mind is now clearer and more inventive than was the case only a few days ago and the lunar high offers you the chance to make the very best of impressions on others.

5 SUNDAY *Moon Age Day 9 Moon Sign Taurus*

With a run of good luck right now, you can afford to back your hunches to a much greater extent than usual. People should be happy to fall in line with your plans and this alone makes life easier and more enjoyable. You project a magnetic personality making others keen to be around you all the time.

6 MONDAY *Moon Age Day 10 Moon Sign Gemini*

Progress at work may be only moderate – or at least that's the way it might seem, but if you are feeling slightly jaded and without much to feel positive about, bear in mind that in reality you may be doing better than you think. At home you may receive some positive input from family members.

7 TUESDAY *Moon Age Day 11 Moon Sign Gemini*

This would be a good time to work with others and to make the most of new opportunities that are definitely on the horizon. With plenty to do and not much time to fit everything don't be tempted to rush your fences. Romance could come knocking on your door around now.

8 WEDNESDAY *Moon Age Day 12 Moon Sign Cancer*

You now enjoy a close bond with friends and may decide to make the present period special, not just for yourself but also for those you are close to. Your mind is occupied with deep thought and you may feel that there are not as many answers as there are questions. Lighten the load with a shopping spree.

9 THURSDAY *Moon Age Day 13 Moon Sign Cancer*

Don't get too tied up with details when it comes to romance but simply let people know how you feel. The lives of people around you may be even more complicated than yours at present and your assistance may be required to steer them in the right direction. Don't be too quick to criticise people at work.

10 FRIDAY *Moon Age Day 14 Moon Sign Leo*

If you have time to spare, make some sensible financial plans. Routines will be comfortable but only if they offer you the chance to stretch your mind. By tomorrow everything will look more dynamic and so today could be good for clearing the decks for action.

11 SATURDAY *Moon Age Day 15 Moon Sign Leo*

Trends suggest that you might be in an argumentative mood today so take care in the way you approach others. This is especially likely in a family setting, so the best-case scenario for you would see you mixing more freely with friends than with family members. Perhaps arrange a long overdue get-together?

12 SUNDAY *Moon Age Day 16 Moon Sign Virgo*

While you are assertive in your dealings with others, you retain a slight element of self-doubt. Don't put this on show to the world at large. You will benefit much more if people view you as extremely positive and sure of yourself. Romance also looks good under present trends, an auspicious trend close to Valentine's Day.

13 MONDAY *Moon Age Day 17 Moon Sign Virgo*

Your work life might be challenging but at least it offers you plenty to think about. Your chart indicates that you will be right on the ball, and your assumptions may turn out to be correct. In every facet of life others will marvel at your ability to get things right first time – to an almost spooky degree.

14 TUESDAY *Moon Age Day 18 Moon Sign Libra*

Just keep following your own path for the moment and don't deviate from it simply to please the sensibilities of people who haven't really any idea what either they or you should be doing. There are some possible romantic opportunities later in the day and friends will prove to be especially important when it comes to planning ahead for fun or travel.

15 WEDNESDAY *Moon Age Day 19 Moon Sign Libra*

It is possible that a previous lack of consideration in your social affairs may come back to haunt you today. Friendships are prone to conflict so take care not to upset someone unintentionally. On the plus side you may find that what you want from life comes easily to you.

16 THURSDAY *Moon Age Day 20 Moon Sign Libra*

You could be in the limelight today, and may attract the attention of your employer or someone you see as potentially important to your future. Taureans who are involved in further education or some sort of training should find this to be an almost ideal period, even if certain colleagues are difficult to deal with.

17 FRIDAY *Moon Age Day 21 Moon Sign Scorpio*

The lunar low comes along and brings a two-day period during which you will have little choice but to sit back and watch, rather than participating in life as much as you would wish. Although this could prove to be slightly frustrating you will at least be getting the rest that your presently active mind craves.

18 SATURDAY *Moon Age Day 22 Moon Sign Scorpio*

It looks as though you will spend a good part of today seeking to please others over yourself. That's par for the course for the moment, but remember that it is only a temporary state of affairs. Make the most of this opportunity to go with the flow as there is a chance that it will lead to some genuine fun.

19 SUNDAY *Moon Age Day 23 Moon Sign Sagittarius*

Focus your attention today on close and intimate relationships. Romance is on the cards for many Taureans and this evening could prove to be extremely interesting, especially if someone close to you has made you a promise. Friends will expect much of you – and they won't be disappointed.

20 MONDAY *Moon Age Day 24 Moon Sign Sagittarius*

Social and travel matters are likely to keep you very busy this week and things start as you mean them to go on – hectic. There could be new beginnings at work with the reorganisation of some kind of job that you haven't been relishing. As things turn out you could be far happier with your lot today than you might have expected.

21 TUESDAY *Moon Age Day 25 Moon Sign Sagittarius*

Material considerations are likely to be less important to you today than inner satisfaction. Of course it's always good to have money but this is a time when you realise that if you are unhappy in life no amount of cash is enough compensation. This realisation might lead you to reprioritise and make more time for social activities.

22 WEDNESDAY *Moon Age Day 26 Moon Sign Capricorn*

Assert yourself creatively today, whether through artistic pursuits or playing to the gallery. It is likely that you will enjoy a little drama more than usual because on a subconscious level you are responding to the fact that you are being watched. Prepare to surprise yourself with your actions and decisions!

23 THURSDAY *Moon Age Day 27 Moon Sign Capricorn*

Today you are surrounded by influences that will help you with practical matters, which is always pleasing to the average Taurean. You can get things done in a flash and you should also be able to get others to follow your lead. The result is likely to be a high degree of personal satisfaction, not to mention a better financial position.

24 FRIDAY *Moon Age Day 28 Moon Sign Aquarius*

There are stresses about today, caused by a conflict between the demands of work and the need for leisure. It may be difficult to make enough time for every commitment but it is necessary. If you want to keep all aspects of your life in harmony you are going to have to work especially hard – though of course you could always call on others for assistance.

25 SATURDAY *Moon Age Day 0 Moon Sign Aquarius*

You will probably see that intimate relationships suit you best today and that casual attachments are less significant. Financially, you may be feeling comfortably off, perhaps partly as a result of the support of your partner. Make sure family members understand fully what you are saying to them.

26 SUNDAY *Moon Age Day 1 Moon Sign Aquarius*

You now have a lot of energy that you can pour into practical and career projects and decisions. Of course the work side of this trend might not be appropriate on a Sunday but that won't stop you finding something concrete to do. Your interest in and enthusiasm for life generally leads you on to better and better prospects.

27 MONDAY *Moon Age Day 2 Moon Sign Pisces*

It is quite easy for you to bring out the best in others this week, which is good because you will need their help and support. There is now more time to talk to people on a deeper level and to find out what really makes them tick. Give some thought to romance because the light of love will be shining in your eyes.

28 TUESDAY *Moon Age Day 3 Moon Sign Pisces*

Trends suggest that you will be getting on well with work colleagues and you are communicative and interesting to have around. This may also prove to be one of the best romantic interludes of the month and when you whisper words of love you are so convincing that nobody could ever doubt you.

♉

March

2017

1 WEDNESDAY *Moon Age Day 4 Moon Sign Aries*

Now you are able and capable of hard work and can do almost anything necessary to get on top of situations. You will enjoy a new burst of energy and can apply yourself to any number of tasks. All the same, remember to take some time out to do whatever takes your fancy.

2 THURSDAY *Moon Age Day 5 Moon Sign Aries*

Ordinary routines may feel like drudgery and there isn't much doubt that you work at your best now when you can choose your tasks for yourself. Learn to delegate if you can because there is no reason why you should have to tackle all the boring jobs yourself. When you allow yourself the time, your mind soars like an eagle.

3 FRIDAY *Moon Age Day 6 Moon Sign Taurus*

Right now you clearly have the knack for success and the lunar high proves to be a very positive driving force. You are ready to work hard to achieve your objectives and won't be held back by the negative responses of some of your colleagues and friends. On the contrary, you can even turn their pessimism to your advantage.

4 SATURDAY *Moon Age Day 7 Moon Sign Taurus*

You are still on a roll and show yourself to be equal to just about any task you choose to take on. There are gains to be made on the financial front and it also appears that you have what it takes to take a prize in the sphere of romance, too. Taureans who have been looking for a new love should keep their eyes open right now.

5 SUNDAY *Moon Age Day 8 Moon Sign Gemini*

Today you may get the right support from the right people. This is partly because you will be keeping your eyes open but mainly because planetary trends are so good in this regard. Don't get too tied down with daily routines but remain flexible, leaving time to do things that come along as a pleasant surprise.

6 MONDAY *Moon Age Day 9 Moon Sign Gemini*

Things do tend to go better in pairs for you today and particularly so when it comes to work considerations. Once the toil is out of the way you might still decide that you need company and will then turn to your friends. Trends indicate that Taurus is not inclined to be family orientated for the moment but that should change closer to next weekend.

7 TUESDAY *Moon Age Day 10 Moon Sign Cancer*

You may find that unconventional answers provide the best match to life's questions right now, and there is little doubt that you are open to originality. You can get most of what you want today simply by tuning your mind to the right frequency and very few people will stand in your way. At least one little victory is more or less certain.

8 WEDNESDAY *Moon Age Day 11 Moon Sign Cancer*

Your social life seems to be on a roll, and it would be good to find time to concentrate on relatives and also people with whom you live. You might not get a great deal of practical things done today, but that doesn't matter because you are likely to be having a really good time.

9 THURSDAY *Moon Age Day 12 Moon Sign Leo*

There are many diverse issues around today and you won't have to work very hard to make life interesting because it manages that of its own accord. Trends suggest a slight tendency for mechanical and electrical devices to let you down at the moment and you may need to use your natural resourcefulness to get around a few setbacks.

10 FRIDAY *Moon Age Day 13 Moon Sign Leo*

Intimate encounters today help to put a new perspective on old issues and you are likely to be very progressive in your general attitudes right now. Get going with new plans and be willing to take on board the alternative strategies of colleagues if you know instinctively that they have a strong chance of success.

11 SATURDAY *Moon Age Day 14 Moon Sign Virgo*

You remain very intuitive and could do much worse than to rely on your gut instinct when dealing with life in a general sense. You may have a great bearing on the actions of friends, and shouldn't underestimate your influence at work either. A few frustrations early in the day should not be allowed to slow you down.

12 SUNDAY *Moon Age Day 15 Moon Sign Virgo*

Take time out during which you can look at your plans for the future and also spend some time talking to family members – particularly about changes you want to make in and around your home. Deal with any feelings of restlessness this weekend by doing something that is new or unusual.

13 MONDAY *Moon Age Day 16 Moon Sign Virgo*

Standard responses probably won't work very well at the moment and it looks as though you will have to find more originality if you really want to get on. Romance may be on the cards and it seems that there are new possibilities opening up that could lead to much happier and more exciting times.

14 TUESDAY *Moon Age Day 17 Moon Sign Libra*

Although today is likely to start out fairly quietly, that is not the way things will remain. As the hours pass, so you find yourself drawn into new projects and involved with both family and friends in little adventures. By the evening you should be ready to paint the town red and any negative feelings from earlier in the day will be gone.

15 WEDNESDAY *Moon Age Day 18 Moon Sign Libra*

This would be a very good moment for a little discretion. The fact is that you might be divulging just a little too much about yourself and your inner thoughts. Not everyone is worthy of your trust so be careful before you say too much. Finances look somewhat stronger around this time, probably as a result of your past actions.

16 THURSDAY *Moon Age Day 19 Moon Sign Scorpio*

You will discover that you have to give way to others under almost all circumstances today and for this you can thank the arrival of the lunar low. Don't be too quick to try to take command and avoid panicking about issues that have no real importance. Someone you don't see often could appear now, possibly with interesting news.

17 FRIDAY *Moon Age Day 20 Moon Sign Scorpio*

It would certainly be best to keep a low profile today and, in particular, to avoid becoming drawn in to pointless and time-wasting family arguments. Stick to frank but tactful honesty and you will find the day goes well for you and by the evening you should be feeling more comfortable and happy.

18 SATURDAY *Moon Age Day 21 Moon Sign Scorpio*

Cultural matters are now favoured as you expand your capacity for communication and your ability to mix with strangers. As a result your social life should become more and more interesting and you might make some new discoveries regarding your own talents. Routines could seem a bit of a chore today.

19 SUNDAY *Moon Age Day 22 Moon Sign Sagittarius*

In a social sense you can benefit from conversations and from listening to what others have to say. Their ideas, when put together with your own, could prove to be extremely useful. A positive attitude towards jobs that need doing around the home can make them go with a swing, though you may still need to get others involved.

20 MONDAY *Moon Age Day 23 Moon Sign Sagittarius*

When it comes to work you are enthusiastic and dynamic. Who could fail to notice that you are around right now? Hardly anyone – although there will always be certain individuals who don't care for you. There is very little you can do about this, so put any worries aside.

21 TUESDAY *Moon Age Day 24 Moon Sign Capricorn*

You should now be in a better position financially, or at least you have ideas in your mind that will increase your fortunes in the not-too-distant future. Taurus can be very ingenious and you certainly won't allow yourself to become stuck with anything that has not proved its productivity. It may help to listen to the ideas of your friends.

22 WEDNESDAY *Moon Age Day 25 Moon Sign Capricorn*

Trends indicate an impatient mood today, so if you really want to get on well accept the fact that you will need to settle down and to allow certain matters to mature naturally. You would also be well advised to let other people do what they understand best, interference will hinder rather than help.

23 THURSDAY *Moon Age Day 26 Moon Sign Capricorn*

All creative pursuits are likely to go well today. This might not be the best day of the month when it comes to making a profit, but then you have to ask yourself whether it is money or happiness that is of utmost importance. You will enjoy a lot of personal satisfaction now, which is worth more than gold.

24 FRIDAY *Moon Age Day 27 Moon Sign Aquarius*

Some situations have to be dug up at the root before you can plant something new and that is what seems to be happening at present. You recognise that there are things you will have to get rid of before you can move on. This inspires a period of spring-cleaning and it won't simply involve sorting through your sock drawer.

25 SATURDAY *Moon Age Day 28 Moon Sign Aquarius*

When it comes to applying yourself practically you just don't cut the mustard this weekend. For this reason alone it would be better to have some fun and to allow a few jobs to wait. If you do insist on taking the reins today you may come to regret it. Relax – the spring is here.

26 SUNDAY *Moon Age Day 29 Moon Sign Pisces*

Avoid needless disagreements with others today by showing your willingness to listen. You can be quite self-willed under present planetary trends and won't always admit that you can be wrong. Keep in touch with relatives and make sure you don't miss an anniversary or event that is of great importance to a loved one.

27 MONDAY *Moon Age Day 0 Moon Sign Pisces*

You are becoming gradually more competitive and show a keener sense of purpose. This is a good thing in most circumstances but it can also get you into a little trouble if you don't temper your present attitude with a degree of diplomacy. In the heat of a discussion it is hard to count to ten before you respond – but you definitely should.

28 TUESDAY *Moon Age Day 1 Moon Sign Aries*

You are now in the middle of a hard working period so accept that there won't be much time for enjoyment – or at least that's the way it looks from your side of the fence. Friends may not understand and might push you to spend more time with them. The real way forward is to make compromises and to leave some work until later.

29 WEDNESDAY *Moon Age Day 2 Moon Sign Aries*

You can now gain either emotionally or financially because you are astute and willing to look at alternative points of view. Your domestic life may also improve as you begin to restructure things and so feel more comfortable with your surroundings. Trends suggest that people from the past could re-emerge around now.

30 THURSDAY *Moon Age Day 3 Moon Sign Taurus*

With a lot of surplus energy, you will have a strong desire to tackle everything at once. Normally the advice would be to slow down but whilst the lunar high is around you can afford to crowd your schedule. A little luck should attend most of your actions and you may also find colleagues and friends gathering around you.

31 FRIDAY *Moon Age Day 4 Moon Sign Taurus*

Physical vitality is still the keynote of the day and your efforts are now geared towards creative activities. This would be a particularly good day for discussions with others because you are so sensible, yet at the same time your aspirations are extremely high. If you don't actually make money today you will be planning how to do so.

♉

April

2017

1 SATURDAY *Moon Age Day 5 Moon Sign Gemini*

Look forward to a fairly agreeable period and one that allows you to get on with whatever takes your fancy. You should not be so busy with necessities at the moment that you have no time to please yourself. Friends are likely to be warm and accommodating and romantic partners may also be especially attentive.

2 SUNDAY *Moon Age Day 6 Moon Sign Gemini*

Under present trends you have a strong thirst for experiences of a new and elevating sort. Intellectual pursuits are what you seek and you may find yourself in just the right sort of company to get the stimulation your mind needs. If you work on a Sunday you could be under a little pressure but most probably of a very positive sort.

3 MONDAY *Moon Age Day 7 Moon Sign Cancer*

Your search for new horizons continues, as does your present willingness to dump a few routines and to get rid of things that are no longer of any use to you. For Taurus this takes courage because you can be a creature of habit. However, you will operate better and react more swiftly if you offload some baggage.

4 TUESDAY *Moon Age Day 8 Moon Sign Cancer*

Your chart suggests that you may be particularly drawn to outdoor interests today. The year is moving on and although it is far from being high summer yet, you would benefit a great deal from some fresh air – both physically and spiritually. Feed your inner self with some stunning views or a brisk walk in the hills.

5 WEDNESDAY *Moon Age Day 9 Moon Sign Leo*

Multi-tasking should be easy for you at the moment. Try out new ideas and get to grips with new technology – like that mobile phone you have never really understood, perhaps! Not only are you good at technical matters, you also seem to be able to see clear through to the core of issues with friends and colleagues.

6 THURSDAY *Moon Age Day 10 Moon Sign Leo*

This could prove to be a less demanding day than you have experienced of late and you won't complain at all about that. Not only will you have more time to look at family issues but you will also know instinctively how to approach even the prickliest of individuals. Most important of all is romance, which blossoms now.

7 FRIDAY *Moon Age Day 11 Moon Sign Leo*

Since your curiosity is so readily aroused right now there is very little going on around you that fails to grab your attention. For once you are willing to listen to all the gossip that takes place within earshot and you will be keen to get involved in all conversations, whether they would normally interest you or not.

8 SATURDAY *Moon Age Day 12 Moon Sign Virgo*

You are now at your best when it comes to practical issues and when you are expected to make up your mind and reach important decisions quickly. With everything to play for in personal attachments you can find the right words of love to sweep someone off their feet and you should also discover a new way to earn money.

9 SUNDAY *Moon Age Day 13 Moon Sign Virgo*

Emotional matters can prove difficult to deal with today, which is why you may divert most of your time and attention in the direction of friendships. Home-based issues will still play a part in your day but in the main you want to be rather less intense than might sometimes be the case. Expect a few social gatherings to be on the cards.

10 MONDAY ☿ *Moon Age Day 14 Moon Sign Libra*

There is assistance around when you need it at the start of this working week and the only real problem is that you might be rather too proud to accept it. Bear in mind that even the stalwart and capable Taurean is only human and there are times when others like you more for admitting you are out of your depth.

11 TUESDAY ☿ *Moon Age Day 15 Moon Sign Libra*

Stand by for another busy and eventful day. It would be sensible to get on with things that can't wait, especially as the next couple of days may be quieter, but you will continue to be on the receiving end of a great deal of support, so make sure you recognise it as such and don't mistake it for interference.

12 WEDNESDAY ☿ *Moon Age Day 16 Moon Sign Scorpio*

The lunar low is likely to slow you down somewhat today but this might not be too much of a problem since you are in a fairly dreamy and sedate state of mind in any case. You rarely get the level of rest you need and this short interlude may well offer you the chance to put your feet up and to let others take the strain.

13 THURSDAY ☿ *Moon Age Day 17 Moon Sign Scorpio*

Now you feel a little frustration because you see events happening around you but won't have much power to intervene. There is now a world of difference between recognising something and having either the tenacity or the strength to address it. Relax because many issues can sort themselves out if you allow them to do so.

14 FRIDAY ☿ *Moon Age Day 18 Moon Sign Scorpio*

Be careful not to be too ambitious just now. The planets presently say that you need to check all details and to move forward slowly and carefully with unfamiliar situations. Family members are likely to be at the forefront of your mind at present, maybe because of the successes they are enjoying.

15 SATURDAY ☿ *Moon Age Day 19 Moon Sign Sagittarius*

Right now it seems you are very eager to please anyone, but especially those who are dear to your heart. Taurus is one of the kinder signs of the zodiac and that certainly seems to be true at the moment. You will shift heaven and earth to do someone a favour and the fact is not lost on them. Stand by to be on the receiving end of some big favours.

16 SUNDAY ☿ *Moon Age Day 20 Moon Sign Sagittarius*

It looks as though there will be new friendships on the way and you will also be quite able to get to grips with a few dodgy issues from the past. At the same time this is a Sunday and should offer you much in the way of enjoyment and diversion. Your intuition is strong and you can easily assess what would please those around you.

17 MONDAY ☿ *Moon Age Day 21 Moon Sign Capricorn*

Not all your attitudes at the moment prove to be orthodox and that could get you into a little trouble with certain people. Nevertheless if you are certain of your ground, stick to what you believe in. Even if you make one or two adversaries on the way such people will come round when they notice your sincerity.

18 TUESDAY ☿ *Moon Age Day 22 Moon Sign Capricorn*

If there is one thing that sets you apart at this time it is your ability to cut through red tape and to see right to the heart of any matter. You prefer things to be simple and uncluttered and will be doing all you can to demystify certain aspects of your life. That won't go down well with those who have an interest in complicating things.

19 WEDNESDAY ☿ *Moon Age Day 23 Moon Sign Capricorn*

Giving and self-sacrifice will motivate you today – though there isn't anything especially unusual about this for a Taurus. In both your vicinity and in the wider world, you are likely to be so moved by the problems of others you will be thinking up practical steps that can be taken to help them out.

20 THURSDAY ☿ *Moon Age Day 24 Moon Sign Aquarius*

You could be somewhat at odds with a particular type of person today. This is because you are always supporting the underdog and you hate unfairness or bullying. Speaking out about injustice is something you can't avoid doing and that could get you into a little bother. Not that the fear of contradiction will worry you at all.

21 FRIDAY ☿ *Moon Age Day 25 Moon Sign Aquarius*

Personal objectives and ambitions are likely to receive small setbacks – but not for very long. In a day or two the Sun moves out of your twelfth solar house and into your first. When it does you can stand by for a great deal more in the way of action and you will soon be more enthusiastic. For the moment just bide your time.

22 SATURDAY ☿ *Moon Age Day 26 Moon Sign Pisces*

You may require some self-restraint in your social dealings, although not because things are likely to be going wrong. On the contrary, the only reason you need to slow things down today is so that you don't totally exhaust yourself. Keeping up with the Jones's might seem very important now – but of course it isn't.

23 SUNDAY ☿ *Moon Age Day 27 Moon Sign Pisces*

Your desire to get ahead gets stronger and stronger – and yet you will still feel that there is something holding you back. Be careful in your dealings with others because there could be someone who is doing their best to lead you up the garden path. Rules and regulations are inclined to get on your nerves at some stage today.

24 MONDAY ☿ *Moon Age Day 28 Moon Sign Pisces*

Influences regarding personal attachments could be somewhat disappointing at the beginning of this particular week. It is likely that certain individuals will let you down and that could lead to more work for you. At the same time you are fairly shrewd and so loss-limitation is part of the Taurean brief right now.

25 TUESDAY ☿ *Moon Age Day 0 Moon Sign Aries*

Stand by for a hectic spell when getting on-side with current news and views can be especially important. Organise your personal schedule as carefully as you can and don't crowd yourself out with unnecessary work. This part of the week is fine for making a financial commitment but think carefully first.

26 WEDNESDAY ☿ *Moon Age Day 1 Moon Sign Aries*

Someone you see very rarely may be getting in touch with you at the moment, and this could send your mind spinning back in time. Part of the reason for your present nostalgia is the Moon, which is now in your solar twelfth house. All of that is out of the window tomorrow as things generally heat up.

27 THURSDAY ☿ *Moon Age Day 2 Moon Sign Taurus*

Changing circumstances can now make your life very much more rewarding. In reality very little is altering, except in your mind, but you can take small developments and turn them to your distinct advantage. The lunar high offers you better luck and more of a tendency to back your hunches to the limit. Colleagues should also be accommodating.

28 FRIDAY ☿ *Moon Age Day 3 Moon Sign Taurus*

This is likely to be another day on which you will want to start new projects and get to grips with all sorts of situations that have been left on the shelf of late. You show yourself to be capable and approachable, which means others are quite willing to go along with your plans. Best of all you could be slightly better off financially.

29 SATURDAY ☿ *Moon Age Day 4 Moon Sign Gemini*

An intimate matter may prove to be rather taxing, creating the feeling that relationships can be more trouble than they are worth. For this reason you might be sticking to casual attachments and even to people who are acquaintances rather than personal friends. Your attitude will soon change and you will revert to your usual kindness.

30 SUNDAY ☿ *Moon Age Day 5 Moon Sign Gemini*

This has to be a good time to go out and make new friends. There are bonuses coming along that will be fed by social activity and you will have little or no difficulty mixing business with pleasure. Keep abreast of what certain family members are up to. This is especially true in the case of younger relatives or those lacking experience.

♉

May

2017

1 MONDAY ☿ *Moon Age Day 6 Moon Sign Cancer*

Today could prove to be slightly trying as far as personal relationships are concerned. It seems as though many situations are custom-made to annoy you, though the problem probably lies within your attitude rather than anywhere else. A little more patience and some genuine diplomacy might help.

2 TUESDAY ☿ *Moon Age Day 7 Moon Sign Cancer*

There are good friends around you at the moment and it is likely to be towards them that you turn for advice or practical help at present. In family matters you will tend to be thoughtful and looking for ways to lend a hand to someone who is too proud to ask for your assistance. A little psychology is called for.

3 WEDNESDAY ☿ *Moon Age Day 8 Moon Sign Leo*

You can find great pleasure in social moments and when you are working hard to please your partner or sweetheart. Events at work may be a little more annoying today, particularly if you are committed to following a course of action that you know to be little more than a waste of time. Taurus is inclined to speak out under present trends.

4 THURSDAY *Moon Age Day 9 Moon Sign Leo*

Although you will be very quick to push your ideas forward at the moment it might be better to be rather more circumspect for a while. What your schemes need is just a little refinement and that won't be possible once they are public property. What you don't want is someone to improve your ideas and then cast them as their own.

5 FRIDAY *Moon Age Day 10 Moon Sign Virgo*

You can use the present period in order to rise to the many career challenges that are likely to be on your mind just at the moment. At the same time you seem to be very busy with ideas that could have a great bearing on your home life. Not everyone will be equally helpful at the moment but it's a fair bet you know how to get what you need.

6 SATURDAY *Moon Age Day 11 Moon Sign Virgo*

Being at home may prove to be most rewarding for you around this time and so you find yourself with a Saturday that is somehow very domestic in nature. In fact this may be a good thing because you will have the chance to sort out a few issues that could have been festering below the surface. People air their opinions and you can too.

7 SUNDAY *Moon Age Day 12 Moon Sign Libra*

You may have a definite desire to please yourself today and there's nothing wrong with that – just as long as you don't ignore those people who are doing their best to make you take notice of them. A little self-indulgence will allow you to catch up on all those half-ideas that have yet to get to the forefront of your mind.

8 MONDAY *Moon Age Day 13 Moon Sign Libra*

You maintain a generally bright and breezy attitude to life and should be more than happy to try something new at any time today. Routines could be something of a bind and you will be doing all you can to avoid them if at all possible. Listen to your intuition, which is strong at present.

9 TUESDAY *Moon Age Day 14 Moon Sign Libra*

It's fine to confide in others, just as long as you know you are dealing with someone who is trustworthy. As a rule you are inclined to play your cards very close to your chest but right now you feel a burning desire to spill the beans. In a romantic sense you sizzle and could be in the mood to sweep someone off their feet.

10 WEDNESDAY *Moon Age Day 15 Moon Sign Scorpio*

This might not turn out to be the most satisfying day of the month for you and it is true that you do have the lunar low to contend with. But it all depends on your expectations and if you are willing to take a break and to rest a little, all should be well. Problems will only arise if you refuse to accept a slower pace.

11 THURSDAY *Moon Age Day 16 Moon Sign Scorpio*

A brief respite is not only advisable – it may prove to be inevitable today. The attitudes of family members are likely to be difficult to understand and it would be better to avoid becoming deeply involved in discussions that seem to have no real purpose. Although you are quite political at present this subject too should be avoided.

12 FRIDAY *Moon Age Day 17 Moon Sign Sagittarius*

Friendship and group activities are once again very much to the fore. Don't forget some sort of celebration that is taking place at any time now and look at your birthday book to make sure you don't forget someone of whom you are very fond. Circumstances may also put you in touch with the dim and distant past.

13 SATURDAY *Moon Age Day 18 Moon Sign Sagittarius*

It would be best today to opt for some light relief if you can. Don't take yourself or anyone else too seriously and be willing to laugh at your own ineptitude. If you do start to look too deeply into life and its peculiarities you could be in for a few less-than-favourable experiences. Be content to browse for day or two.

14 SUNDAY *Moon Age Day 19 Moon Sign Sagittarius*

You could be in two minds about a plethora of situations today because you are simply not as sure of yourself as would sometimes be the case. Acting on impulse may not usually be your thing but it could work out quite well at the moment. Romantic partners might be hard to understand but can offer some fascinating insights all the same.

15 MONDAY *Moon Age Day 20 Moon Sign Capricorn*

Try for a little break from obligations if possible today. For once you simply don't want to think incessantly about the needs that life has of you but rather break free and find ways to enjoy yourself. There ought to be people around who would be more than willing to join in your temporary truancy from responsibility.

16 TUESDAY *Moon Age Day 21 Moon Sign Capricorn*

It is important today to emphasise what you believe to be true, even if other people have different ideas. If minor difficulties occur, they won't matter in the long run. Your integrity is one of your most important possessions and you are famous for it. Friends will support your plans around this time.

17 WEDNESDAY *Moon Age Day 22 Moon Sign Aquarius*

Move swiftly today because under present planetary trends this is certainly not a time to let the grass grow under your feet. Success may result from being in the right place to make things happen and this is as important in your social life as it will be at work. Romance is also likely to pay a visit around now.

18 THURSDAY *Moon Age Day 23 Moon Sign Aquarius*

You remain quite happy to be on the move and not in the least interested by thoughts of resting. All the same there ought to be time to get a little luxury into your life, and you should also have some time to make a special fuss of your partner. Your wit and sense of humour are most important right now.

19 FRIDAY *Moon Age Day 24 Moon Sign Pisces*

Intuitive in your response to personal attachments, you shouldn't have any trouble working out why those you love are behaving in the way they are. This gives you the chance to be one step ahead of them and to do things that will please them no end. A high degree of kindness is evident all round and that should be very welcome.

20 SATURDAY *Moon Age Day 25 Moon Sign Pisces*

Don't get too carried away with your own big ideas today because although under normal circumstances these tend to be very useful and effective, little problems seem to arise all the time right now. Accept help and support from people who are in the know and you can mitigate any real difficulty.

21 SUNDAY *Moon Age Day 26 Moon Sign Pisces*

It's time to explore the wider world beyond your door and planetary trends now will incline you towards travel and adventure. This would be an excellent time to take a holiday or even any short trip that stimulates your mind and exercises your body. You are very much in tune with your environment at the moment and it really shows.

22 MONDAY *Moon Age Day 27 Moon Sign Aries*

You should have plenty of opportunities to increase your overall influence, especially at work. In a social sense you are now more willing to accept a slightly less dominant role and you should also be happy to try something new that demands a level of learning on your part. Taurus is slightly less assertive today.

23 TUESDAY *Moon Age Day 28 Moon Sign Aries*

Where business and practical matters are concerned life is likely to be going very much the way you would wish at this stage of the week. Many things tend to come together under present planetary trends, with the assistance of friends and superiors. Being in the right place also certainly helps.

24 WEDNESDAY *Moon Age Day 29 Moon Sign Taurus*

Money-wise your efforts now are likely to prove very successful and the lunar high brings a breath of fresh air into your life as far as new possibilities are concerned. Socially speaking you are likely to be extremely active and your increasing popularity with others is bound to give you more confidence and the chance to make advances.

25 THURSDAY *Moon Age Day 0 Moon Sign Taurus*

A time when you fulfil your own expectations and show the world what you are capable of, often without a great deal of effort on your part. Although there are limits to your capabilities at the moment you will have to work very hard in order to find them. Friends should be especially approachable now.

26 FRIDAY *Moon Age Day 1 Moon Sign Gemini*

The desire for new mind-broadening experiences remains especially strong at the moment, but brings with it the possibility of boredom unless you allow yourself a degree of personal freedom. Things will still get done eventually, even if you don't tackle everything today. Try to be with people you find exciting and stimulating.

27 SATURDAY *Moon Age Day 2 Moon Sign Gemini*

You would benefit from some emotional self-discipline in order to get on as well as you would wish today. On a strictly practical level it would be too easy to invest funds into situations that look rather odd from the start. Keep your purse or wallet tightly closed until at least tomorrow, after which true bargains are more likely.

28 SUNDAY *Moon Age Day 3 Moon Sign Cancer*

You now have excellent insight and won't have any difficulty at all working out how others are likely to react under any given circumstance. This can be very useful and it means that you may even be able to manipulate situations in your favour. If your partner has been behaving somewhat oddly of late, now is the time to find out why.

29 MONDAY *Moon Age Day 4 Moon Sign Cancer*

Your present strong intuition is even more in evidence today and is a commodity that can help you no end. This is a great period for sharing your deepest feelings and emotions and your insight into the way those around you are likely to react to any situation is quite remarkable. This is Taurus at its best and almost everyone will notice.

30 TUESDAY *Moon Age Day 5 Moon Sign Leo*

New material interests are likely to be coming along all the time and many of them have genuine value and profit. You are less likely to be making mistakes now and the general good fortune of this month shows itself. Don't be stuck in one place today for any longer than is strictly necessary.

31 WEDNESDAY *Moon Age Day 6 Moon Sign Leo*

If loved ones seem to be putting you under pressure you will need to steady things down by talking calmly and rationally. You cannot afford to become involved in family arguments. It would be all too easy to be drawn into rows that have nothing to do with you in the first place. Distance yourself and wait for things to blow over.

♉

June

2017

1 THURSDAY *Moon Age Day 7 Moon Sign Virgo*

You seem to be a fairly dominant force in a social sense because it is you who will be coming up with all the good ideas and making most of the arrangements. Not everything you have in mind will please your whole circle of friends so select those of a similar mind-set to you for your chosen activities.

2 FRIDAY *Moon Age Day 8 Moon Sign Virgo*

Opt for the bright lights of the social world whenever you can at the end of this week. The year is advancing and you will want to make the most of the early summer and the opportunities it offers for new and exciting adventures. Taurus is now at its optimistic best and you will also be less fussy than is often the case.

3 SATURDAY *Moon Age Day 9 Moon Sign Virgo*

Teamwork matters today and if you are willing to get involved with a new group of people who seem to have the same sort of ambitions as you do, the result could eventually be electrifying. Get to grips with new technology around this time and seek some help with gadgets you don't understand. A younger family member might help.

4 SUNDAY *Moon Age Day 10 Moon Sign Libra*

Certain choices today will prove to be extremely rewarding and the only difficulty will be choosing which way to jump under any given circumstance. For this you can rely upon your intuition, which remains well honed at present. Don't be surprised if you discover you have an unexpected admirer.

5 MONDAY *Moon Age Day 11 Moon Sign Libra*

The fun period is likely to continue but anyone can have too much of a good thing and Taurus is definitely no exception. In amongst all the laughter and general frivolity you are painfully aware that there are practicalities to address. You are not being a wet blanket just because you spend at least part of today getting on with something real.

6 TUESDAY *Moon Age Day 12 Moon Sign Scorpio*

You can't really avoid repeated delays and setbacks today and tomorrow and the irritant is the arrival of the lunar low. Since there is very little you can do to change things, settle down and find ways round problems. This will most likely involve getting others to work steadily on your behalf.

7 WEDNESDAY *Moon Age Day 13 Moon Sign Scorpio*

Things are still not looking wonderful but you are one of the most resilient people to be found throughout the length and breadth of the zodiac. In your need to find new ways to solve old problems you should be able to impress both yourself and the world at large. All in all what happens today proves just how ingenious you can be.

8 THURSDAY *Moon Age Day 14 Moon Sign Sagittarius*

There may be a few challenges around at the moment but you are in the right frame of mind to approach these head on. Acting on impulse is one option, but it is far more likely that you will be lining up your intellectual weapons in order to deal with matters in your own inimitable way. Friends should be supportive but relatives may not be.

9 FRIDAY *Moon Age Day 15 Moon Sign Sagittarius*

Keep abreast of local news and views, whilst at the same time staying well in touch with national and world affairs. An informed Taurus is a more successful one and you can prove yourself to others through the sheer power of your knowledge at the moment. This stands you in good stead when advancement is offered.

10 SATURDAY *Moon Age Day 16 Moon Sign Sagittarius*

Since domestic situations can cause you a few irritations this weekend and also bearing in mind the advancing summer, it is away from your home that you tend to turn at present. Look for some excitement and if nobody else has any good ideas, think one or two up for yourself. Anything would do, as long as it's not routine.

11 SUNDAY *Moon Age Day 17 Moon Sign Capricorn*

Today may throw up matters about which you have little personal understanding, but such is the quality of your nature that nobody would ever guess it. Using what you do know, together with your instincts, you can steer a careful path and impress a wealth of people on the way. Stand by for a slightly slower period that lies in store.

12 MONDAY *Moon Age Day 18 Moon Sign Capricorn*

Your power and effectiveness may not be all that you would wish. This is partly because you feel yourself hampered by the attitudes and actions of those to whom you are usually so close. When people behave strangely, give them space and do something else instead. The more diverse you make today, the better it will be.

13 TUESDAY *Moon Age Day 19 Moon Sign Aquarius*

Since self-serving attitudes and the fulfilment of personal desires seem to mean very little to you now, you will most likely get more from looking after others instead. The greatest enjoyment you are likely to discover now comes from knowing that you have been of service to people who are very much in need of your support.

14 WEDNESDAY *Moon Age Day 20 Moon Sign Aquarius*

Don't believe everything you hear today and be willing to stand back from situations before you commit yourself. This is an ongoing trend and is very important, if only because you are being relied upon. It's a great responsibility at times to be a Taurean but it's something you take seriously and you hate to get things wrong.

15 THURSDAY *Moon Age Day 21 Moon Sign Aquarius*

On a practical level you now need to be getting as much done as you can. Handling half a dozen different jobs at the same time is child's play to you at the best of times, and certainly now presents no problem at all. People generally seem to favour your ideas and will want to involve you in lengthy discussions about new possibilities.

16 FRIDAY *Moon Age Day 22 Moon Sign Pisces*

Any sort of contact at a professional level is likely to work out well, though you may have slightly more difficulty in personal situations and attachments. The week is growing older and if there is something you have been meaning to get done ever since Monday, this is the time to get on with it. Enlist some support for social incentives.

17 SATURDAY *Moon Age Day 23 Moon Sign Pisces*

You need excitement, adventure and a real challenge this weekend but you won't find any of these things by sitting in a chair and waiting. All the incentives are yours to take and you should find that your friends and family members are only too willing to fall in line with whatever takes your fancy. Love is strengthened no end today.

18 SUNDAY *Moon Age Day 24 Moon Sign Aries*

Today there could be plenty of news arriving and most of it is likely to be good. Intellectual pursuits of one sort or another are just the thing to make you feel as though you are alive and competitive whilst at the same time you need change and diversity. Expect a very busy period and a time of potential rewards.

19 MONDAY *Moon Age Day 25 Moon Sign Aries*

There are gains to be made today but you should also register it as being a fairly quiet time, since the Moon now occupies your solar twelfth house. You need to be sure of yourself when it comes to romantic attachments but a little variety and the ability to react according to changing circumstances is also necessary.

20 TUESDAY *Moon Age Day 26 Moon Sign Taurus*

You show yourself to be a larger than life character now and there are certain people around who are likely to be surprised by the person you presently seem to be. Taurus people are a little unusual in that they appear to be quiet and contemplative but when the planets line up well – look out world!

21 WEDNESDAY *Moon Age Day 27 Moon Sign Taurus*

You can probably have it all at the moment, or at least as much of life as you can take in at one moment. The lunar high makes you keen to get ahead and offers you all the incentives necessary to make a big impression when it matters the most. Try to find some time in amongst all the activity to please yourself and to have genuine fun.

22 THURSDAY *Moon Age Day 28 Moon Sign Gemini*

Life might now feel fairly humdrum as you attempt to get things organised. You may not be inspired to push yourself when you are in or around your home and your best chance of livening things up is to get out of doors. Why not take a trip? Even the change of air would make you feel wonderful.

23 FRIDAY *Moon Age Day 29 Moon Sign Gemini*

Once again try a total change of scenery today if you have the chance to get one. Restlessness prevails, and discussions of one sort or another are inclined to fall flat. You simply won't be on sparkling form for much of today but you can certainly help yourself by not hanging around and vegetating.

24 SATURDAY *Moon Age Day 0 Moon Sign Cancer*

You can get the most from life today by being flexible in your attitude and by avoiding disputes, especially with family members. Love comes knocking at your door this weekend – though there is some doubt as to whether you will be keen to make the most of it. Creature comforts will be of little importance.

25 SUNDAY *Moon Age Day 1 Moon Sign Cancer*

Setting great store by your own ideas is fine but that doesn't mean you can afford to ignore what others are saying. If you at least pay lip service to their opinions you will avoid offering any offence and your path will run more smoothly. Avoid becoming involved in problems you already know to be insoluble.

26 MONDAY *Moon Age Day 2 Moon Sign Leo*

Communications in the career world are ever more important around now and the more you express your ideas, the better is the response you will get. Your confidence remains generally high and with a planetary peak on the way it looks as though you are about to enter one of the best periods for some time. Make the most of it.

27 TUESDAY *Moon Age Day 3 Moon Sign Leo*

Trends suggest that you can afford a more freewheeling attitude so get out and about and make the most of the advancing summer. You love the better weather and the chance it offers for you to break routines and to feel the warm winds on your face. Don't stick to one place today.

28 WEDNESDAY *Moon Age Day 4 Moon Sign Leo*

All meetings should be highly rewarding at this stage of the week though it has to be said that you probably won't be in the mood for too much work. That's because there are so many other fascinating possibilities about, all of which look far more interesting than boring old routines. Socially it's off with the old and on with the new.

29 THURSDAY *Moon Age Day 5 Moon Sign Virgo*

This is a great time to be with others and probably the best time of the year so far for taking a holiday. The larger the group in which you are involved the better you will feel and Taurus is definitely in the mood to share almost anything. Even if you are still as cautious as usual regarding money, someone will be able to prise it from you.

30 FRIDAY *Moon Age Day 6 Moon Sign Virgo*

All of a sudden what you are seeking is not so much excitement and new experiences but rather intellectual companionship and meaningful conversation. The last day of June puts you in touch with your deeper self and you will be wide open to the influence of those who can help you open your mind to a different view of life.

♉

July

2017

1 SATURDAY *Moon Age Day 7 Moon Sign Libra*

It seems that the chance to do things for other people will make you happy today. There's nothing especially strange about this but what is different is the fact that you may not even know the people concerned. The charitable side of your nature is much enhanced by present planetary trends and is open to any potential good cause.

2 SUNDAY *Moon Age Day 8 Moon Sign Libra*

While making progress and getting things done is what keeps you generally cheerful today, you will also be feeling your responsibility to others quite keenly. Relationships in the workplace could be a little strained and you should do all you can to get things back on to a more even keel. Your social impulses will be strong.

3 MONDAY *Moon Age Day 9 Moon Sign Scorpio*

Put duties and demands to one side and instead of fighting against the lunar low, learn to embrace it. If you first of all accept that this is not the time for advancement or progress, you will then settle back and enjoy what life is offering in quieter ways. No planetary aspect or period is bad – it's all down to the way we approach them.

4 TUESDAY *Moon Age Day 10 Moon Sign Scorpio*

It's time to take stock and to plan carefully for what is likely to be taking place towards the end of this week. Your general level of confidence might not be quite as high as you would wish but that need not hold you back. Most of what is happening at the moment takes place in your head.

5 WEDNESDAY *Moon Age Day 11 Moon Sign Scorpio*

Don't be too quick to criticise others over issues you may not fully understand yourself. Instead of finding fault, pitch in, co-operate and lend a hand to sort things out. You can have a great deal of fun at the moment by pooling your resources with others and by maintaining a positive attitude.

6 THURSDAY *Moon Age Day 12 Moon Sign Sagittarius*

Your ego receives a boost, most of which come as a result of the compliments that come your way from those around you. If gadgets go wrong at home you will have to tell yourself that nothing lasts forever and shell out to replace them. Before you do however, look around for a bargain.

7 FRIDAY *Moon Age Day 13 Moon Sign Sagittarius*

Certain issues at work are going to demand your attention to such an extent that you won't have as much time as you would wish to spend with loved ones or friends. The problem is that even when you are not actually at work it is still likely to be on your mind. Try to relax, if only for short periods.

8 SATURDAY *Moon Age Day 14 Moon Sign Capricorn*

Try for a temporary respite from duties and demands, whilst getting someone else to take some of the pressure from you with regard to responsibilities at home. Delegation is an art and it's one that you don't always understand. Present trends assist you to trust others to do things capably and well.

9 SUNDAY *Moon Age Day 15 Moon Sign Capricorn*

You are likely to be very confident within yourself under present planetary trends and that has to be good as far as your life as a whole is concerned. Things go wrong for Taurus when it is apprehensive about both the present and the future but you exude so much confidence at present that you also enjoy a great deal of optimism.

10 MONDAY *Moon Age Day 16 Moon Sign Capricorn*

There seems to be a strong social boost on the way at the start of this working week and there are also planetary trends around that will put you in touch with some fairly unusual sorts of people. Some of these will be individuals you already know but you are also likely to be making new friends around now. Long-term plans can also be addressed at present.

11 TUESDAY *Moon Age Day 17 Moon Sign Aquarius*

Don't believe everything you hear today because it is quite obvious that some of the comments that come your way may be misleading. Fortunately you should be able to shrug these off and remain objective and shrewd. It's also your responsibility to keep friends safe from themselves at present.

12 WEDNESDAY *Moon Age Day 18 Moon Sign Aquarius*

It is intellectual pursuits that you look for now and you certainly will not be impressed by any task that is either dirty or unsavoury. If you seem to be quiet when viewed by others they might think you are either depressed or sulking. For this reason it is important to tell people that you are simply in a reflective frame of mind.

13 THURSDAY *Moon Age Day 19 Moon Sign Pisces*

This is a time during which family issues should be working out rather well for you. Career developments are also likely and you may well be in line for some sort of advancement. Since it is clear that you are being watched a good deal by your bosses right now it would be sensible to be on your best behaviour.

14 FRIDAY *Moon Age Day 20 Moon Sign Pisces*

Pleasant encounters with others seem to be the order of the day and as the weekend grows closer you might already be in a frame of mind that turns your attention away from the strictly practical. You need diversion and your ready mind is already thinking of ways in which you can entertain yourself and those around you.

15 SATURDAY *Moon Age Day 21 Moon Sign Aries*

Extended negotiations and major decisions make for an interesting if fairly complicated sort of Saturday. In group situations you may feel the need to help others reach a consensus – something that is often important to Taurus. You remain at all times tactful, diplomatic and honest.

16 SUNDAY *Moon Age Day 22 Moon Sign Aries*

You will now find greater success than ever when it comes to winning over social contacts. New friends are the result and you will be mixing with the sort of individuals who stimulate your intellect. There are likely to be few obstacles in your path today and you enjoy a fairly smooth ride through life.

17 MONDAY *Moon Age Day 23 Moon Sign Aries*

Rules and regulations, which are generally your meat and drink, are now inclined to get on your nerves. This leaves you feeling somewhat frustrated with yourself, particularly so because a twelfth house Moon is making you somewhat quieter and less reactive than usual. The result will be a few frustrations, which a friend can help to dispel.

18 TUESDAY *Moon Age Day 24 Moon Sign Taurus*

You may decide that today is the day for some excitement – though in reality life itself will probably provide this for you. With the Moon in your sign you are likely to be filled with enthusiasm and will be happy to go for something newer, brighter and better. Just watch how well everyone else fits in with your plans at present.

19 WEDNESDAY *Moon Age Day 25 Moon Sign Taurus*

This is definitely the right moment to be moving ahead with life and you have what it takes to do something amazing right now. In company you now tend to keep up a very high profile and you know what it takes to be noticed. Romantically speaking you exhibit all the charm necessary to knock someone for six!

20 THURSDAY *Moon Age Day 26 Moon Sign Gemini*

Contacts with friends should be especially favourable today and therein lie the seeds of your own progress. It is the ideas of those around you that turn out to be the most potentially successful and you will be getting on well with all manner of people. Later in the day there is likely to be room for a return to a more romantic interlude.

21 FRIDAY *Moon Age Day 27 Moon Sign Gemini*

Time spent with your lover is likely to be both rewarding and enjoyable today. You may also be in the mood for a change of scene and so if it is possible to take a day off, this is the time to do it. The more you stimulate your mind, the greater are the possibilities for advancement. There are still strong romantic possibilities around.

22 SATURDAY *Moon Age Day 28 Moon Sign Cancer*

There is now conflict between your personal ambitions and what you feel to be your obligations and it will be quite difficult to fit in everything you know you should accomplish. Because of this you need to think long and hard and then to only do those things you know are not going to create waves. It won't be easy but you can win out.

23 SUNDAY *Moon Age Day 0 Moon Sign Cancer*

Socially speaking this period ought to turn out to be very encouraging. You are getting to know new people and forming deeper alliances with people who were only acquaintances before. Finding common ground with others is now much easier than it was and you may have some new, unexpected, friends.

24 MONDAY *Moon Age Day 1 Moon Sign Leo*

For much of the time today you coast along merrily and it will seem as if all sorts of situations are sorting themselves out for once. Taurus is used to having to struggle for what it gets, though it has to be said that for much of the time this is really just a state of mind. If you really feel yourself to be successful – then you will be!

25 TUESDAY *Moon Age Day 2 Moon Sign Leo*

There may be various ups and downs this week and some of them start today. It could be necessary to think on your feet more than you have been doing recently but that won't bother you because it increases the level of excitement you encounter on your path through life. Newer and better professional possibilities are likely.

26 WEDNESDAY *Moon Age Day 3 Moon Sign Virgo*

Today you are not likely to be pushing yourself or your plans more than is strictly necessary. All the same your capacity for solid hard work knows no bounds. There are few calls on your time that do not in some way improve your lot in life and you should feel that certain obligations are now slipping into the background. Friends will be attentive.

27 THURSDAY *Moon Age Day 4 Moon Sign Virgo*

Advancement is likely as a result of improving your social connections. Don't give in today if the going gets tough because that is just the time to put in your maximum effort. All sorts of people seem to favour your success today and even if it's for reasons of their own they are quite willing to help you along.

28 FRIDAY *Moon Age Day 5 Moon Sign Libra*

Stand by your decisions today when you have made them and don't allow yourself to be diverted from any path you have chosen. People will be trying to talk you round but your intuition is strong so use your own judgement. Today is good socially and brings further new opportunities.

29 SATURDAY *Moon Age Day 6 Moon Sign Libra*

Unexpected delays are likely to be the hallmark of this particular weekend but you may find that these actually lead to some exciting and even productive results. You can't judge any book by its cover right now so remain alert and open to new possibilities. Spend some time with loved ones, too.

30 SUNDAY *Moon Age Day 7 Moon Sign Libra*

Expand your range of intellectual interests around now as almost anything can stimulate your imagination. You demonstrate a positive and forward-looking attitude though take care to register the impact that your ideas have on family members. In sporting activities you are likely to excel.

31 MONDAY *Moon Age Day 8 Moon Sign Scorpio*

You need diplomacy and co-operation today if you are going to reach longed-for objectives but fortunately you are also likely to be putting in that famous Taurean effort again. When you pool your resources with colleagues and friends there is no end to what you can achieve and sharing is not only useful now but also enjoyable.

♉

August

2017

1 TUESDAY *Moon Age Day 9 Moon Sign Scorpio*

This is a good time for gathering the sort of information that could feather your nest in the immediate future. Nothing escapes your attention now and you will be especially good at working out the underlying motivations of people close to you. Spend some special time with your partner today.

2 WEDNESDAY *Moon Age Day 10 Moon Sign Sagittarius*

This ought to be a fairly inspirational sort of day and one during which you will be gathering together all sorts of information that may or may not turn out to be useful in the short and medium-term. Very little escapes your attention at the moment and you have what it takes to turn even the most insignificant details to your advantage.

3 THURSDAY *Moon Age Day 11 Moon Sign Sagittarius*

Look out for some completely new and unique ideas at this time. Not all of them are coming from you personally but if you keep your ears and eyes open you may learn a lot from those around you. In a co-operative mood, any sort of partnership should flourish under present planetary trends.

4 FRIDAY *Moon Age Day 12 Moon Sign Sagittarius*

Give yourself a pat on the back for a success that comes your way today – probably inspired by your actions some time ago. However, this is no time to be complacent because there is plenty more to do and a wealth of possibilities in the pipeline. This will be especially true for self-employed Taureans.

5 SATURDAY *Moon Age Day 13 Moon Sign Capricorn*

Things continue to be generally good for you through the weekend but this might not be the best time to start any new project that is going to demand all of your time and attention. Rather you will relish doing a bit here and little there, scratching around the farmyard of life and gaining information and entertainment wherever you find it.

6 SUNDAY *Moon Age Day 14 Moon Sign Capricorn*

There is likely to be a great sense of purpose today, together with a feeling of lightness and frivolity. It might seem that conflicts arise as a result but this isn't the case. The present planetary picture allows you to get exactly what you want without having to apply much pressure to either people or situations.

7 MONDAY *Moon Age Day 15 Moon Sign Aquarius*

In a social sense there ought to be plenty of opportunities for enjoyment this week and it all starts today. You will be chatty, forthcoming and very interesting to know. Generally speaking this is one of the best times of the year to show others exactly what makes you tick and this is important because Taurus can sometimes be a little quiet.

8 TUESDAY *Moon Age Day 16 Moon Sign Aquarius*

It looks as though this is the right time to concentrate on the practical and financial side of life – even though it is quite plain that you also want to carry on enjoying yourself. For some there is the chance of a journey that is purely for pleasure, whilst other Bulls will simply be staying in the 'counting house'.

9 WEDNESDAY *Moon Age Day 17 Moon Sign Pisces*

Home and family are under the planetary spotlight both today and for a couple more days to come. It might seem that everyone is demanding your attention at the same time but you are well able to keep up and in any case you will be secretly pleased that people need you so much. All the same don't be taken for granted.

10 THURSDAY *Moon Age Day 18 Moon Sign Pisces*

Your career is now aided by your ability to draw on knowledge that even you didn't know you possessed. You are a little like a vacuum cleaner when it comes to amassing information, all of which you eventually put to good use. People will call you ingenious and in some ways you are, so simply smile and accept the compliment.

11 FRIDAY *Moon Age Day 19 Moon Sign Pisces*

You will most likely want to end the working week with a flourish but don't use up all your energy during the day because the evening could be especially exciting. If you have nothing specifically planned for the hours after work, get thinking early in the day. What shows more than anything now is your rising popularity.

12 SATURDAY *Moon Age Day 20 Moon Sign Aries*

Look towards cash this weekend because there are ways and means by which you can make yourself better off. Once again your ingenuity is the key and you deal with numbers and mathematical problems quite easily at present. In addition to acquiring more money you might also enjoy finding new ways to spend some of it.

13 SUNDAY ☿ *Moon Age Day 21 Moon Sign Aries*

With a slightly quieter day in store you should have time to think a good deal and to retreat into your own little world much more than has been the case recently. This may turn out to be an entirely fortunate state of affairs because you have been burning the candle at both ends for a few days.

14 MONDAY ☿ *Moon Age Day 22 Moon Sign Taurus*

Most of your energy goes into your work this week and you might find that you now have less time for socialising. There is assistance around if you are willing to accept it but chances are that you are feeling quite independent. Friends should be especially warm and kind today and tomorrow.

15 TUESDAY ☿ *Moon Age Day 23 Moon Sign Taurus*

Your mind and intelligence don't let you down at the moment and you relish the prospect of taking on any sort of problem that taxes your grey cells. These might be related to your work or simply for entertainment – it doesn't really matter. Don't get bogged down with pointless details or fruitless tasks.

16 WEDNESDAY ☿ *Moon Age Day 24 Moon Sign Gemini*

It seems as if everything you undertake at the moment is working out pretty much the way you would wish but this isn't happening as a result of good luck. Rather it is thanks to the advanced planning you did some time ago and also responds to your own positive state of mind right now. Romance is likely to be in evidence.

17 THURSDAY ☿ *Moon Age Day 25 Moon Sign Gemini*

The smooth running of everyday life is something that always appeals to you because even when you need change and adventure you don't always welcome them. For now you can be reasonably sure that things will work out as you expect and it is clear that you have a good understanding of what is needed in order to get ahead.

18 FRIDAY ☿ *Moon Age Day 26 Moon Sign Cancer*

Today could be ruled by romance – that is if you were not a generally practically minded son or daughter of Taurus. Still you will notice how much positive attention is coming your way and if you have been looking for a new relationship this is as good a time as any to get things moving. Emotions are strong but often under lock and key.

19 SATURDAY ☿ *Moon Age Day 27 Moon Sign Cancer*

You have very winning ways and because you appear approachable and humble all sorts of people will be doing anything they can to help you out. Don't be too quick to take offence over a disagreement with a colleague or friend. What they are trying to tell you is very likely to be for your own good in the end.

20 SUNDAY ☿ *Moon Age Day 28 Moon Sign Leo*

There is little doubt that it is your mind that matters the most for the moment. Although you can still make satisfactory progress in your life generally you are in a thoughtful frame of mind and inclined to spend a long time mulling things over. This phase is quite natural and even necessary so although you might get restless, in reality you shouldn't.

21 MONDAY ☿ *Moon Age Day 29 Moon Sign Leo*

You are very fortunate in your choice of friends at present because so many of them actively want to help you all they can. Not that you will need their assistance from a practical point of view. Things are going better than you could possibly imagine and you will get an inkling today that certain situations are turning in your favour.

22 TUESDAY ☿ *Moon Age Day 0 Moon Sign Virgo*

Don't jump into things as a means of escape from situations that don't appeal to you. Better by far at the moment to face up to the realities of life. Once you do so, apply yourself and sort out anything that needs immediate attention. In a day or two you should be far more optimistic than you are now.

23 WEDNESDAY ☿ *Moon Age Day 1 Moon Sign Virgo*

Social and group relationships should put a definite smile on your face today and you have what it takes to get ahead, especially at work. Your powers of reasoning are especially good and you can sort out complicated details that will have other people in a real spin. When it matters the most you come up with extremely good ideas.

24 THURSDAY ☿ *Moon Age Day 2 Moon Sign Virgo*

Now you are brimming over with energy and should be enjoying this wonderful time in every way possible. If you are on holiday then so much the better because you will have the time to open your eyes and to see what a great world it can be. In particular you will enjoy nature in all its diversity.

25 FRIDAY ☿ *Moon Age Day 3 Moon Sign Libra*

When it comes to professional matters you should take care not to impose your will on others. If you lead by example rather than trying to talk your way through situations, people will respect you all the more. With the weekend ahead you may already be planning something fascinating for yourself and your lover.

26 SATURDAY ☿ *Moon Age Day 4 Moon Sign Libra*

This could be one of the best days of the month for career developments – which makes it something of a pity that it arrives on a Saturday when many people are not at work. In a social sense you will be quite happy to go with the flow but what you should not do this weekend is sit around waiting. The time for action has arrived – at least for today.

27 SUNDAY ☿ *Moon Age Day 5 Moon Sign Scorpio*

No matter how hard you try today it is unlikely that you will be able to make as much headway in life as you would wish. This isn't a problem as long as you realise that you are merely going through a two-day lunar low, which is a time better spent recharging your batteries than trying to get ahead against insurmountable odds.

28 MONDAY ☿ *Moon Age Day 6 Moon Sign Scorpio*

Be true to yourself and your values but don't push issues until you force an argument. It would be far better at the moment to simply allow things to ride rather than getting involved in unnecessary conflict. None of this will be a problem at all if you simply go with the flow and accept what life offers.

29 TUESDAY ☿ *Moon Age Day 7 Moon Sign Sagittarius*

This is a good day for Taurus on a personal level. Your ego and confidence are both strong and you really believe that you have what it takes to make a difference. At the same time you also have very high standards and there may be occasions when others find it difficult or even impossible to keep up with you. Socially life is good.

30 WEDNESDAY ☿ *Moon Age Day 8 Moon Sign Sagittarius*

Material matters are now much enhanced and you remain very enterprising in your outlook. You will be taking more of a chance from a financial point of view but any risks you do take are likely to be very calculated ones. There is now little to stand in your way but in some respects you would rather relax than work too hard.

31 THURSDAY ☿ *Moon Age Day 9 Moon Sign Sagittarius*

What matters most at the moment is that you are busy and fulfilled in your daily life. Feeling useful is also very important and you can turn your hand to almost anything. Creature comforts will become significant towards the evening, though if the sun shines you might choose to take a break earlier in the day.

September

2017

1 FRIDAY

☿ *Moon Age Day 10 Moon Sign Capricorn*

Your thinking processes are now like lightning and you should definitely do all you can to make others listen to what you have to say. There is no point in being a shrinking violet because even if it seems at first that you have to bulldoze your ideas across, in the end people may be glad that you spoke out so directly.

2 SATURDAY

☿ *Moon Age Day 11 Moon Sign Capricorn*

Information that comes in today could be arriving from just about any direction and you need to be on the ball when it comes to getting things done. You have so much energy right now that even the most trying of tasks will be out of the way in a flash. And when work is done and finished you can have fun!

3 SUNDAY

☿ *Moon Age Day 12 Moon Sign Aquarius*

Your mind works swiftly at the moment, which might mean that you take the decisions while those around you dither. People will recognise your confidence and might rely on you heavily for advice and practical assistance. Don't be afraid to get to grips with a somewhat difficult personal issue.

4 MONDAY

☿ *Moon Age Day 13 Moon Sign Aquarius*

You should enjoy the kind of company you are keeping at the moment and can expect an interesting and stimulating week ahead. Not everyone will be on your side at first but you clearly have what it takes to talk people round in a diplomatic and sensitive way. Jobs will be out of the way in a flash.

5 TUESDAY ☿ *Moon Age Day 14 Moon Sign Aquarius*

Today you are likely to find the greatest happiness at home, probably lost in a world of concepts and possibilities. A lot of information may be coming your way at the moment and that alone can prove to be the greatest fascination for you. Don't be too surprised if your partner does something that is quite out of character.

6 WEDNESDAY ☿ *Moon Age Day 15 Moon Sign Pisces*

Beneficial influences surround joint finances right now and you could do worse than to discuss the family budget with your partner or other family members. To some people this would be the bore of the week but Taurus likes to have things sewn up and is never happier than when sorting out the future – especially in a monetary sense.

7 THURSDAY ☿ *Moon Age Day 16 Moon Sign Pisces*

Along comes a time of significant energy – one in which you are determined to take back command of situations over which you seem to have lost control. Be certain of the moves you make on the financial front and once you have made up your mind about anything, stick to it, no matter what.

8 FRIDAY ☿ *Moon Age Day 17 Moon Sign Aries*

Personal finances are likely to be on your mind today and you might feel in the mood to organise your money in order to make sure that there will be enough cash around at the end of this year. That probably means that you already have your eye on the Christmas period – perhaps because you have something very special planned this year.

9 SATURDAY ☿ *Moon Age Day 18 Moon Sign Aries*

It is really important today to make up your mind to a particular course of action and then to stick to it, even if those around you are inclined to disagree. It's a fact that you will be at odds with certain people at the moment, no matter what you do to try to put the situation right. For this you can thank the present planetary line-up.

10 SUNDAY ☿ *Moon Age Day 19 Moon Sign Taurus*

In a changed planetary picture from yesterday, today your ideas are as attractive to others as they are to you. Your confidence inspires others to follow your lead. In your romantic life you now have what it takes to knock someone for six – even if you were reluctant to try before.

11 MONDAY ☿ *Moon Age Day 20 Moon Sign Taurus*

The quicker you make up your mind about something today, the better it is likely to work out for you. The lunar high makes you positive and decisive – in fact in just the right frame of mind to make a success of almost anything. You should be particularly fortunate at the moment when it comes to making money.

12 TUESDAY ☿ *Moon Age Day 21 Moon Sign Gemini*

An exciting day when it looks as though you will continue to have great influence in the world you have helped to create. Someone might not agree with either your point of view or your planned actions but that doesn't really matter because in the end you can bring them round in a very positive way.

13 WEDNESDAY *Moon Age Day 22 Moon Sign Gemini*

In a domestic sense you can expect a period of great co-operation and should be surrounded by family members who seem only too willing to follow your lead. This might surprise you so much that you become somewhat transfixed and will show yourself to be just as kind and giving as can be.

14 THURSDAY *Moon Age Day 23 Moon Sign Cancer*

There are strong domestic impulses around right now and although you might be rushed off your feet in the practical world you will still find time to be kind and attentive to those you love the most. Don't allow yourself to be too tied to conventions of any sort and show your originality.

15 FRIDAY *Moon Age Day 24 Moon Sign Cancer*

You are at your best when surrounded by those you love and trust but there is a slight tendency at the moment for you to be rather suspicious about one or two individuals. Although you can occasionally be too negative for your own good, trends suggest that your present concern might not be misplaced.

16 SATURDAY *Moon Age Day 25 Moon Sign Cancer*

Use today to rise to certain challenges in your life. Trends suggest that you might also have decided that the time is right to make some changes in your relationships. Circumstances make you quite positive but maybe just a little ruthless at the moment, so exercise a little caution so that you don't upset others.

17 SUNDAY *Moon Age Day 26 Moon Sign Leo*

Take advantage of your personal freedom and relish the chance to do your own thing, even if you have to reorganise a busy schedule in order to make this possible. Look out for opportunities to travel and to learn anything new that will help to broaden your horizons and outlook. This is no time to hesitate.

18 MONDAY *Moon Age Day 27 Moon Sign Leo*

You will feel at your happiest today when you are enjoying the more carefree side of your life. Although you will be quite willing to get your head round practical matters, in the main you feel like letting go of responsibility and simply enjoying what the day has to offer. Everything will soon be back to normal so for now try to have fun.

19 TUESDAY *Moon Age Day 28 Moon Sign Virgo*

It's fine to be on the move and to travel today, just as long as you know you have completed things that can't wait. It is necessary to get your priorities right, something that isn't usually an issue for you. It's rare that anyone would accuse you of shirking your responsibilities but they might well do so around now.

20 WEDNESDAY *Moon Age Day 0 Moon Sign Virgo*

An intellectual peak comes your way and you will be at your best when involved in the world of philosophy and new ideas. As you look around you, there may be occasions when you notice something that could be better. Now you are more likely to do something about these situations, either verbally or even with a screwdriver.

21 THURSDAY *Moon Age Day 1 Moon Sign Libra*

You have a strong desire to meet new and interesting people, and maybe even to get in touch with someone you see as being very important or even famous. You may also feel inclined to write to friends, especially those who live far away. You have plenty to say for yourself, either via text message, the internet or letters.

22 FRIDAY *Moon Age Day 2 Moon Sign Libra*

The time is right to take a little break from obligations. Perhaps your sense of adventure comes to the fore and you wish to escape into a different world for a while? People you come into contact with casually have interesting things to say and this could lead to further ideas of your own. A little time on your own later would do you good.

23 SATURDAY *Moon Age Day 3 Moon Sign Scorpio*

Take stock of your affairs today and by all means keep on planning but don't commit yourself to firm arrangements or sign any documents. The lunar low might take the wind out of your sails in a social sense and it seems likely you will be content with your own company for the moment.

24 SUNDAY *Moon Age Day 4 Moon Sign Scorpio*

There might be a tendency for you to get caught up in one small problem after another today and it would be best all round if you left some of the worrying to others. You do more than your fair share as a rule and so it is only right that you let others take the strain now and again. Think up something really inspirational to do instead.

25 MONDAY *Moon Age Day 5 Moon Sign Scorpio*

Broaden your horizons in any way you can and be open to new experiences today. Many of the rewards you reap right now come whilst you are on the move and there won't be a lot of time for thinking on the way. Instead, rely heavily on your intuition and your own special awareness.

26 TUESDAY *Moon Age Day 6 Moon Sign Sagittarius*

This looks likely to be a dynamic and probably a tense time when it comes to your closest attachments. It may be hard to judge how others will react to situations and you kick yourself when you realise you have got things wrong. Despite these difficulties you should still be enjoying a good ride in a business sense.

27 WEDNESDAY *Moon Age Day 7 Moon Sign Sagittarius*

A time of busy social activity and the start of the autumn will find you anxious to get on well with almost everyone. New personalities are likely to enter your life now and there are gains to be made as far as your finances are concerned. Attitude is all-important when it comes to anything educational.

28 THURSDAY *Moon Age Day 8 Moon Sign Capricorn*

The time has come to exploit a career opportunity or a new idea. You will be both practical and efficient when it comes to negotiating the business side of your life but less competent in social matters – where things could be going slightly wrong. Fitting everything in is going to be a struggle today and something may just have to wait.

29 FRIDAY *Moon Age Day 9 Moon Sign Capricorn*

You may be dealing with a matter you see as quite serious today, even though in the longer-term it is probably nothing of the sort. It may also – reluctantly – be necessary to think about cutting a specific tie. You can be a real creature of habit so the thought of a significant change may scare you a little.

30 SATURDAY *Moon Age Day 10 Moon Sign Capricorn*

The more variety and change you get into your life today and during the weekend, the happier you will feel about life in a general sense. This is the perfect time to talk and even to get yourself involved in deep and meaningful discussions. Your intellectual ability right now fits you well for any sort of puzzle or quiz.

October

2017

1 SUNDAY *Moon Age Day 11 Moon Sign Aquarius*

Some matters in your life need careful consideration and Sunday may well offer you the time you need to sit down and mull things over. This doesn't mean you will be inactive all day. On the contrary you are still very much in the mood for improving your home in a number of ways and heaven help anyone in the family who won't lend a hand.

2 MONDAY *Moon Age Day 12 Moon Sign Aquarius*

You are likely to be very opinionated at the moment and although that can be good in terms of getting your own way, it probably won't make you quite as popular as you can sometimes be. No matter what happens it would be sensible to retain a little diplomacy and to use some tact when dealing with important people.

3 TUESDAY *Moon Age Day 13 Moon Sign Pisces*

You could find finances easier to deal with today than of late, maybe because your partner or family members are taking your advice in some way. You should also be enjoying a few indulgences under present trends and will be attracted to anything luxurious. Try to make your home welcoming now.

4 WEDNESDAY *Moon Age Day 14 Moon Sign Pisces*

With lots to keep you occupied it looks as though today will be fast and furious. If anything you will need more time to fit in everything you want to do. Much of what you undertake at the moment is likely to be away from home, though tomorrow will present a very different picture.

5 THURSDAY *Moon Age Day 15 Moon Sign Aries*

Grasp any chance to broaden your intellectual horizons with both hands as the pace of life gradually increases throughout today. Learning experiences will be very welcome and no matter what your age it will be possible for you to make some stunning realisations. The adage 'you're never too old to learn' is especially true now.

6 FRIDAY *Moon Age Day 16 Moon Sign Aries*

Since you seem to be at some sort of mental peak right now your persuasive talents are present in great measure. You can put these to excellent use when it comes to business or even family matters. Save some time for simple enjoyment and avoid becoming so involved in paradoxes and conundrums that you fail to enjoy yourself.

7 SATURDAY *Moon Age Day 17 Moon Sign Taurus*

This is definitely the right time to impress someone with your ideas and know-how. The lunar high makes you naturally dominant, aspirational and good to know. Winning others round is no problem at all and you should discover that you have what it takes to be a real leader – even if you sometimes don't know where you are going!

8 SUNDAY *Moon Age Day 18 Moon Sign Taurus*

You should be able to accomplish a lot today, most of it without undue effort. While you often work hard to achieve your objectives you now have what it takes to make others work hard on your behalf. It looks as though you won't be afraid to stand up for the rights of anyone you want to support.

9 MONDAY *Moon Age Day 19 Moon Sign Taurus*

This ought to be an especially productive period as far as your finances are concerned and you won't have any trouble at all getting others to follow your lead when it comes to monetary matters. You are wise and, not always typical of Taurus, careful and even frugal in your spending. Be prepared for friends to be a little vague in their responses to you.

10 TUESDAY *Moon Age Day 20 Moon Sign Gemini*

Communication with others may be marred by arguments today, even if you are not the one who is causing the problems. Such situations only hamper progress you now want to make, which is why you will be loath to become involved. If necessary, spend most of today working on your own.

11 WEDNESDAY *Moon Age Day 21 Moon Sign Gemini*

Although there are now likely to be unexpected demands placed upon you, the chances are that you will take this in your stride. A little patience may be required with people who seem determined to frustrate your efforts but you have a great capacity at present to laugh and shrug your shoulders.

12 THURSDAY *Moon Age Day 22 Moon Sign Cancer*

Although today should still be very enjoyable there could be a slight tendency for you to get carried away with your own big ideas. There is plenty of help around when you need it and probably also some timely advice. The problem is that you don't always listen as much as you should – and difficulties could be the result.

13 FRIDAY *Moon Age Day 23 Moon Sign Cancer*

Capitalise on any new information gleaned from social gatherings. Look forward to plenty of activity, much of which is inspired by you in the first place. There might not be as much time for work as you would wish but when it comes to enjoying yourself the sky is the limit, both now and during the upcoming weekend.

14 SATURDAY *Moon Age Day 24 Moon Sign Leo*

You throw yourself into the thick of things in an everyday sense and will get necessary tasks going like clockwork. Part of your skill lies in your ability to get others to follow your lead and even to work on your behalf. At your tactful best you can instruct almost anyone – without them realising that it is happening.

15 SUNDAY *Moon Age Day 25 Moon Sign Leo*

There may be some changes and alterations to take on board and this might mean having to react quickly to life – possibly in a way that makes you feel a little uncomfortable. Actually it will do you no harm at all to be put on the spot and if nothing else you will prove to yourself that you are more than capable of reacting to circumstances.

16 MONDAY *Moon Age Day 26 Moon Sign Virgo*

When it comes to your social life you can create a powerful impression right now and few people will fail to notice your presence. Friends and colleagues will appreciate your forthright manner and that they know exactly how you feel about situations. People you don't know so well could find you a little pushy.

17 TUESDAY *Moon Age Day 27 Moon Sign Virgo*

Meetings with others may inspire you with new ideas and feed your intellect no end. If you have the sort of job that brings you into contact with people then so much the better. As far as your personal life is concerned you continue to feel happy with your lot but you may be faced with certain family members who are not.

18 WEDNESDAY *Moon Age Day 28 Moon Sign Libra*

What seems to matter the most today is your ability to communicate with friends and family members. As far as your partner is concerned it appears that you are now able to explain yourself much better than was the case over the last couple of days. Pleasing the most important person in your life is now of paramount importance.

19 THURSDAY *Moon Age Day 29 Moon Sign Libra*

Trends suggest that you continue to be motivated by material issues and you will be doing all you can to make sure that the months ahead are positive, especially from a financial point of view. As far as today is concerned you will be slightly less inclined to concern yourself with petty worries or irritations.

20 FRIDAY *Moon Age Day 0 Moon Sign Libra*

Instead of moving in the direction of others you now have what it takes to bring them to you. Because you are a little less inclined to travel or to seek out new places for now, you sit for a little while at the centre of your own universe. Those who need you will have to seek you out – which they certainly will.

21 SATURDAY *Moon Age Day 1 Moon Sign Scorpio*

Certain plans could receive something of a setback and you have to acknowledge the presence of the lunar low, even if you would rather just push on as usual. You might feel the urge to indulge yourself in some way and since other planetary trends indicate that you will be especially close to family members, your home really counts now.

22 SUNDAY *Moon Age Day 2 Moon Sign Scorpio*

Although things are nowhere near as busy as they were a couple of days ago, you can relish the peace and quiet that has suddenly descended on you. For some it will be as if you are resting in the eye of a hurricane because no matter how much is whizzing around you, very little of it seems to have a bearing on you personally.

23 MONDAY *Moon Age Day 3 Moon Sign Sagittarius*

Your desire to consolidate your position is of paramount importance to you now. Material matters should appear to be in better shape than they have been for quite a while, though a great deal of this has to do with your present attitude. In other words nothing much has changed except the way you view your life.

24 TUESDAY *Moon Age Day 4 Moon Sign Sagittarius*

Finances should look stronger today and there is no doubt that you are looking very seriously at improving your lifestyle in some way. Taurus is now drawn towards luxury and there may be moments today when you revel in the chance to spoil yourself. The only slight drawback is that to do so might cost you something.

25 WEDNESDAY *Moon Age Day 5 Moon Sign Sagittarius*

Close ties are your most rewarding area today and you are really turning on the charm in order to please the most important person in your life. Emotions run close to the surface and you are likely to speak your mind to a greater extent when it comes to expressing your true feelings. This will be much appreciated by your lover.

26 THURSDAY *Moon Age Day 6 Moon Sign Capricorn*

There is still a tendency for you to spend more money on indulgences than you would as a rule. At the same time you are also better at bringing more cash in, so your overall bank balance probably won't change very much. This is a good time to enhance your physical surroundings and to make relatives more comfortable too.

27 FRIDAY *Moon Age Day 7 Moon Sign Capricorn*

Current trends definitely favour information gathering and there is not a single stone on the path of your life that you won't want to turn over. This stands you in good stead and means you are not likely to miss anything of importance. Since you are still very exacting you may have to work on your own because others can't keep up.

28 SATURDAY *Moon Age Day 8 Moon Sign Aquarius*

Today brings swift progress and a realisation that things are going your way as far as the practicalities of life are concerned. You continue to be very careful but you can finally put paid to any recent delays and should feel that you are positively cruising along. This probably won't be a day for social niceties.

29 SUNDAY *Moon Age Day 9 Moon Sign Aquarius*

Now is the time to gain a distinct advantage over anyone you view as a competitor. You don't have to be ruthless to get ahead because instead you rely on consistency and a willingness to keep going when others fall by the wayside. In the end you have what it takes to prove yourself time and again, as everyone knows.

30 MONDAY *Moon Age Day 10 Moon Sign Pisces*

You are now determined to make money, even to the extent that you might be looking at the possibility of a part time job or some form of speculation that looks as though it could pay off handsomely. Don't fall for get-rich-quick schemes – although someone would have to be very good to fool an Earth sign such as you.

31 TUESDAY *Moon Age Day 11 Moon Sign Pisces*

Getting together in discussion with colleagues and friends can now work to your distinct advantage, even though there are bound to be one or two people involved that you don't care for. Who knows? With a little patience and perseverance on your part you could get to know a former adversary better and end up liking them a great deal.

November

2017

1 WEDNESDAY *Moon Age Day 12 Moon Sign Pisces*

It could be that you are putting across your point of view a little forcefully at this stage of the week and in all honesty you would get on better if you relaxed more. Hang fire with certain projects and ideas while you get existing jobs out of the way. If you don't crowd your schedule you will remain more relaxed and better to know.

2 THURSDAY *Moon Age Day 13 Moon Sign Aries*

Not everyone will appreciate the fact that you are speaking your mind today and if there are any difficulties regarding your outspoken manner, these are likely to be at work. In other spheres of your life things are going to be very different because from a social point of view everyone you meet is interested in your opinions.

3 FRIDAY *Moon Age Day 14 Moon Sign Aries*

Your grip on your finances may be a little tenuous now. It's not that anything is likely to be going wrong – more that you don't recognise the sort of momentum regarding money that makes Taurus happy. In a personal sense you have what it takes at the moment to bring extra zip into your romantic life.

4 SATURDAY *Moon Age Day 15 Moon Sign Taurus*

This is a time during which you ought to be putting more faith in Lady Luck. This doesn't mean taking ridiculous chances with cash but rather that you could take a little chance with something non-financial. A better attitude becomes possible when you are dealing with an old, difficult family issue.

5 SUNDAY *Moon Age Day 16 Moon Sign Taurus*

New initiatives in the romantic department for some Taurus subjects could lead to a very interesting and maybe even a fairly surprising sort of Sunday. If you have been looking for a new relationship, this is one of the times of the year to keep your eyes open. First dates should work out well but established attachments are good too.

6 MONDAY *Moon Age Day 17 Moon Sign Gemini*

You may meet someone exciting today who will challenge your preconceptions and get you thinking along radical new lines. Be careful though because important information could go astray at the worst possible time. That's why it is very important to check and double check the post, your mobile phone and email messages today.

7 TUESDAY *Moon Age Day 18 Moon Sign Gemini*

Professional developments could seem to be rather hard going and for that reason you might have to rely more on the help and advice of colleagues. This won't go down especially well if you have been in open competition with one or two of them but despite yourself you could make a new friend as a result of your present needs.

8 WEDNESDAY *Moon Age Day 19 Moon Sign Cancer*

This is a good day during which to be in the social mainstream and you should get a wonderful response from almost anyone you come across. Not that you are leaving anything to chance at the moment. On the contrary you are filled with a desire to check and double-check all details, which is great for you but could annoy someone.

9 THURSDAY *Moon Age Day 20 Moon Sign Cancer*

You should discover that loved ones at home now have what it takes to make you more comfortable in some way. Fix something that is broken, or at least get someone else to do it for you, and don't put up with second best in anything. Taurus is now at its organisational best and won't settle for anything less than perfection.

10 FRIDAY *Moon Age Day 21 Moon Sign Leo*

Romantic affairs are now even more positively highlighted, but the accent looks likely to be on secret relationships in the case of some Taureans. Try as hard you can to keep your attachments out in the open because clandestine meetings are likely to leave you feeling both guilty and somehow less honest. Find friends in whom you can confide.

11 SATURDAY *Moon Age Day 22 Moon Sign Leo*

It looks as though you are now in for a period of great nostalgia, which is not unusual as the nights become longer and winter really takes hold. Seek out your favourite people this weekend, but resist any temptation to hide at home. Friends could prove to be just as important to you now as family members.

12 SUNDAY *Moon Age Day 23 Moon Sign Virgo*

Right now there are likely to be some very pleasurable encounters taking place and this is definitely a Sunday during which you need to take time out for personal enjoyment. Who knows what awaits you out there in the big, wide world? You have to be there to recognise the possibilities so get out of bed early and take part.

13 MONDAY *Moon Age Day 24 Moon Sign Virgo*

You seem to be very tuned-in to the emotional state of those with whom you interact today. This will be especially true in the case of your partner or loved ones but is also the case in more casual relationships. People are likely to be receptive to your sensitivity and single you out for their confessions.

14 TUESDAY *Moon Age Day 25 Moon Sign Libra*

It looks as though you will be feeling generous today, and this won't just be a case of throwing a pound or two into the nearest charity tin. On the contrary you might put yourself out significantly in order to help people you recognise as being in emotional pain or distress. You can even be of help in some ways that you will never realise.

15 WEDNESDAY *Moon Age Day 26 Moon Sign Libra*

Despite your present mental dexterity you might recognise within yourself a certain flightiness and unreliability. This won't delight you at all because it runs contrary to your mental self-image. But although it won't please you, it could be a source of some small amusement to others and makes you appear all the more human to them.

16 THURSDAY *Moon Age Day 27 Moon Sign Libra*

You will now enjoy making frequent excursions and for those Taurus subjects who have decided to take a very late holiday the choice will prove to have been very fortuitous indeed. A great many situations will seem to sort themselves out and that leaves you with more time to explore possibilities that haven't occurred to you before.

17 FRIDAY *Moon Age Day 28 Moon Sign Scorpio*

With the lunar low comes what might turn out to be the quietest and least eventful time you will experience during November. If you can't make any headway, then you might as well take a break. A few tasks that probably seemed necessary yesterday now take their place at the back of your mind as you realise they are not really urgent at all.

18 SATURDAY *Moon Age Day 0 Moon Sign Scorpio*

Some matters will be a little off-course as you continue to lack the necessary energy to wade into life with your usual appetite. On the contrary, you are likely to leave quite a few things to colleagues and friends, whilst you adopt a sort of dreamy attitude. This is quite natural and even crucial for Taurus from time to time.

19 SUNDAY *Moon Age Day 1 Moon Sign Sagittarius*

The pleasure principle is strong but beware a slight tendency to spend too much and to become too fond of luxury. It has to be remembered that yours is an Earth sign, and this alone means that you can be something of a hedonist. Try a spoonful of moderation, though it is a medicine you won't care for today.

20 MONDAY *Moon Age Day 2 Moon Sign Sagittarius*

The greatest benefits today come through teamwork and your ability to make everyone around you feel indispensable. The kindest and most considerate side of Taurus is now on display and it is a character that almost everyone loves. You won't forget a kindness and will repay each instance handsomely.

21 TUESDAY *Moon Age Day 3 Moon Sign Sagittarius*

A little versatility is what you require today, especially when keeping in mind your desire to get ahead. You may discover talents you didn't know you had but can also expect to come up against a few obstacles on the path to success. At some stage during the day you will require some time to yourself.

22 WEDNESDAY *Moon Age Day 4 Moon Sign Capricorn*

Present planetary influences bring out the best in you when it comes to communicating with those around you. You want to be in touch with as many people as possible and will use every means at your disposal to make sure you are in the know. Listen carefully because the smallest comments can prove to be helpful.

23 THURSDAY *Moon Age Day 5 Moon Sign Capricorn*

Today you will be exchanging ideas with others and talking as much as possible to individuals who have it in their power to help you along. Don't get tied down with pointless routines and be sure that you keep your schedule open for last-minute events. Being flexible is the most important factor at this time.

24 FRIDAY *Moon Age Day 6 Moon Sign Aquarius*

You will probably find that family interests are very much to the fore today. Much of your attention is likely to be focused on making sure that those you love are comfortable and have whatever they need. In your own life you will discover how important it now is that you have a place for everything and a plan for each contingency.

25 SATURDAY *Moon Age Day 7 Moon Sign Aquarius*

You appreciate the emotional responses of others today and should definitely be in the market for romance. The commitment you show to your partner – or maybe someone you wish was your partner – ensures that they respond positively. Finances are likely to look better too and you could receive some unexpected cash.

26 SUNDAY *Moon Age Day 8 Moon Sign Aquarius*

This is likely to be a time for smooth sailing in all negotiations and discussions with family and friends. Your attention to detail might not be all you might wish but that doesn't really matter because most of the details of life will sort themselves out. You will get on particularly well at the moment with those you consider to be efficient.

27 MONDAY *Moon Age Day 9 Moon Sign Pisces*

You may be in the dark regarding a particular plan of action and could feel left out of negotiations that have a great part to play in your future. Trends suggest that you should beware of reacting harshly. Things may not be what they seem and it would be all too easy to over-react without thinking first.

28 TUESDAY *Moon Age Day 10 Moon Sign Pisces*

It might seem as though your general popularity has peaked and you could feel as though you don't have the level of influence in the world that you did only a week or so ago. Actually nothing much has changed, except your own particular point of view. Concentrate instead on specific tasks for today and tomorrow.

29 WEDNESDAY *Moon Age Day 11 Moon Sign Aries*

You show your ability to be a natural diplomat at this time and should be able to get almost anyone to follow your lead. This is achieved with just a dash of coercion and a great deal of encouragement. You could find that you are taking a middle path between warring factions but make sure you don't get personally involved.

30 THURSDAY *Moon Age Day 12 Moon Sign Aries*

Good luck helps you to achieve some of your objectives, whilst others are accomplished because of your ability to focus and to work hard. Merely agreeing or disagreeing with those around you won't be enough today because you will be expected to take the lead in most areas of life. People trust you implicitly now.

♉

December 2017

1 FRIDAY *Moon Age Day 13 Moon Sign Taurus*

All the deep thinking of the last couple of days can now be turned to your advantage as the lunar high gives you boundless energy and a very cheerful attitude to life generally. This is a time for fresh starts and for taking a few chances. You should also be feeling fairly good from a physical point of view and able to work extremely hard.

2 SATURDAY *Moon Age Day 14 Moon Sign Taurus*

Get an early start this morning with all-important projects and new starts. Fate will be ready to lend you a helping hand and you might enjoy the added bonus of a little good fortune. Almost everyone you meet will be easy to deal with, accommodating and the best that they can be.

3 SUNDAY ☿ *Moon Age Day 15 Moon Sign Gemini*

Private and intimate matters seem to be far more interesting and rewarding today than public appearances of any sort. Taurus tends to be quite secretive at the moment and you will only share your innermost feelings with a very small selection of people. Take care though, because some people could think you are sulking or scheming.

4 MONDAY ☿ *Moon Age Day 16 Moon Sign Gemini*

It will be possible to discover someone's true feelings today and no matter what you have been told in the past there is more to learn right now. You may have to delve quite deeply in order to get to the bottom of things, but you are certain to find the effort worthwhile. Friends should be happy to have you along in social situations.

5 TUESDAY ☿ *Moon Age Day 17 Moon Sign Cancer*

You seem to have great control over your working life at this time and will not be in the least fazed when someone tries to give you more responsibility. On the contrary this is something you are likely to welcome. However, before you rise to the challenge, maybe you should ask yourself if you will be better off as a result.

6 WEDNESDAY ☿ *Moon Age Day 18 Moon Sign Cancer*

Family relationships are now likely to be very cordial and even where there has been a little tension of late you should be able to establish a lasting truce. Certain people don't annoy you as much as they normally would, but this has more to do with your present tolerance than it has to do with their behaviour.

7 THURSDAY ☿ *Moon Age Day 19 Moon Sign Leo*

Practical matters and general run-of-the-mill situations run smoothly, whilst at the same time you turn towards new projects and different ways of addressing old problems. Friends may be constantly seeking your attention, most likely because they recognise how much they can rely on you.

8 FRIDAY ☿ *Moon Age Day 20 Moon Sign Leo*

Your desire to please others – which is genuine at present – could fall flat if they refuse to allow you into their world. Don't be too worried about this because in a few days things should be back to normal. Instead of dwelling on things keep yourself busy and think up a new way to deal with issues that have been troubling you for a while.

9 SATURDAY ☿ *Moon Age Day 21 Moon Sign Virgo*

It would be a mistake to believe everything you hear today because there are some people around who will be doing all they can to mislead you. It takes someone very clever to get one over on the average Taurus, but you might be just a little easier to fool at present. In the main you will be feeling fairly quiet today.

10 SUNDAY ☿ *Moon Age Day 22 Moon Sign Virgo*

You now make things happen, both inside and outside of work. Also of significance is the fact that your popularity is about as high as it can get. That means you are flavour of the month, even to people you don't normally get on with too well. You should also expect to be doing rather better in the financial stakes.

11 MONDAY ☿ *Moon Age Day 23 Moon Sign Virgo*

It seems to be your specific know-how that helps you to get on at work and there isn't any doubt that specialist skills are worth most to you today. Concentrate on those things you know that others don't because people are likely to be relying heavily on you. You can shine like a star in all social settings both today and for some days to come.

12 TUESDAY ☿ *Moon Age Day 24 Moon Sign Libra*

Every job you do at the moment may be a one-off and so needs extra thought. That won't bother you at all because you remain as methodical as always, yet somehow more ingenious and adventurous. Away from practicalities, grasp any chance to do something completely different, most likely with your partner.

13 WEDNESDAY ☿ *Moon Age Day 25 Moon Sign Libra*

Communication remains especially important and it is within your social interactions that you get your greatest joys at the moment. You may have a dawning realisation of just how close it is to Christmas, but being the sort of person you are you won't panic about it. Rather you will sit down and make a plan for yourself.

14 THURSDAY ☿ *Moon Age Day 26 Moon Sign Scorpio*

It will probably be necessary to keep one or two plans on ice until the lunar low passes and leaves you with a greater chance of success and more energy. Don't be too quick to take on extra responsibilities or to begin sorting out something very complex to do with family members. Your level of patience will not be as high as usual.

15 FRIDAY ☿ *Moon Age Day 27 Moon Sign Scorpio*

Whilst you may not be succeeding as much as you would wish in the outside world, you can build an interesting and diverting world inside your own head. Taurus is very dreamy at the moment, which incidentally will not please you very much. But we all need to visit our own personal fantasy worlds from time to time – especially Taurus.

16 SATURDAY ☿ *Moon Age Day 28 Moon Sign Scorpio*

You should now be getting the best of all worlds from domestic matters, whilst at the same time continuing to be very practical in the way you approach life. Although you could have an urge to get out and about today, thoughts of Christmas and the final arrangements you have to make could keep you tied to your home.

17 SUNDAY ☿ *Moon Age Day 29 Moon Sign Sagittarius*

You are unlikely to be making snap decisions today but will be thinking things through very carefully indeed. That's your way right now and though it doesn't always impress other people, you can't avoid this side of your nature. It looks as though you will be showing ever more concern for certain individuals who are worse off than you are.

18 MONDAY ☿ *Moon Age Day 0 Moon Sign Sagittarius*

Communication with influential people could prove to be worth a good deal to you at this time and it seems as though you come across interesting types all the time. At work you might have to stand up for your rights more than usual – that is if you don't want colleagues to be either stealing your thunder or else using your ideas.

19 TUESDAY ☿ *Moon Age Day 1 Moon Sign Capricorn*

If you have any problems being objective about a particular matter today it would be sensible to ask an outsider – someone who has no vested interest either way. At least that way you will get an impartial point of view and one on which you can most probably rely. This would be a good time to make a real fuss of your partner.

20 WEDNESDAY ☿ *Moon Age Day 2 Moon Sign Capricorn*

You will be expected to make some fairly heavy compromises at the moment and that isn't going to be easy. The fact is that Taurus can be very stubborn, especially so when its most cherished values are at stake. Before digging your heels in today it is worth analysing how important your pride really is.

21 THURSDAY ☿ *Moon Age Day 3 Moon Sign Capricorn*

Prepare yourself to make a very good impression on almost everyone today. You manage to achieve that delicate balance between getting things done while at the same time contributing to the Christmas spirit. At some times today you will even be playing the fool – a situation that definitely delights others and which proves to be entertaining.

22 FRIDAY ☿ *Moon Age Day 4 Moon Sign Aquarius*

It may feel today as if everyone is getting on better than you are but this is nothing but an illusion. Be content with your lot and spend at least some of today looking forward to Christmas Day. The festive season is just around the corner so relish the fact and throw yourself into the seasonal atmosphere.

23 SATURDAY *Moon Age Day 5 Moon Sign Aquarius*

It looks as though you will now be making the best of specific beneficial trends that stand around you. Although you are warm, sincere and friendly, it is towards the practical aspects of life that your mind is most likely to turn. Many Taureans would relish a shopping spree today – even though the stores will be very crowded.

24 SUNDAY *Moon Age Day 6 Moon Sign Pisces*

Don't overestimate the strength of character that you possess – or your ability to put important new plans into action, despite the arrival of Christmas. By this evening you might feel ready for a rest but the demands of a family life, together with the party atmosphere of Christmas Eve should ensure you don't get much.

25 MONDAY *Moon Age Day 7 Moon Sign Pisces*

High spirits prevail and with planetary influences about that make you far less inclined to take yourself at all seriously, you may well shock one or two people with your antics. Personal attachments flourish under present trends and it looks as though you will find ever better ways to express both your love and your passion.

26 TUESDAY *Moon Age Day 8 Moon Sign Pisces*

You continue to show a great appetite for life and will now be looking for new things to do and alternative positive actions to take. Some Taureans could become just a little restless if there seems to be nothing to do except eat and drink, so look for ways to occupy your intellect and enjoy being on fine form socially.

27 WEDNESDAY *Moon Age Day 9 Moon Sign Aries*

Today is good for intimate relationships and for promoting a greater sense of harmony within your home. Romance can flourish under prevailing trends and all sorts of compliments could be coming from directions you might not have expected. Stand by to make this part of the holidays seem really special for all concerned.

28 THURSDAY *Moon Age Day 10 Moon Sign Aries*

Along comes a busy period with a definite tendency towards movement and travel. Maybe you are visiting relatives at a distance or else enlivening the holidays by going somewhere special. Whatever you decide to do today it should be something that is as far away from normal routines as you can possibly manage.

29 FRIDAY *Moon Age Day 11 Moon Sign Taurus*

Today marks the start of a most progressive phase for you and if there is any frustration at all around right now it will come from not being able to move forward in the way you would wish. Instead of bemoaning this fact use the lunar high to push forward more home-related ambitions. Good luck is on your side at this time.

30 SATURDAY *Moon Age Day 12 Moon Sign Taurus*

If there are obstacles in your path today, carry on regardless of them. There are times at the moment when standard responses won't work and that's where your present ingenuity will need to come in. Get together with people you don't see much during the year and make the most of social encounters to further your own ideas.

31 SUNDAY *Moon Age Day 13 Moon Sign Gemini*

Practical common sense dominates your life on this New Year's Eve. You feel the need to get on with something useful and will do so, even if your actions go against the grain as far as certain other people are concerned. Fortunately you are also quite diplomatic at present and so can find ways to get round awkward types.

RISING SIGNS FOR TAURUS

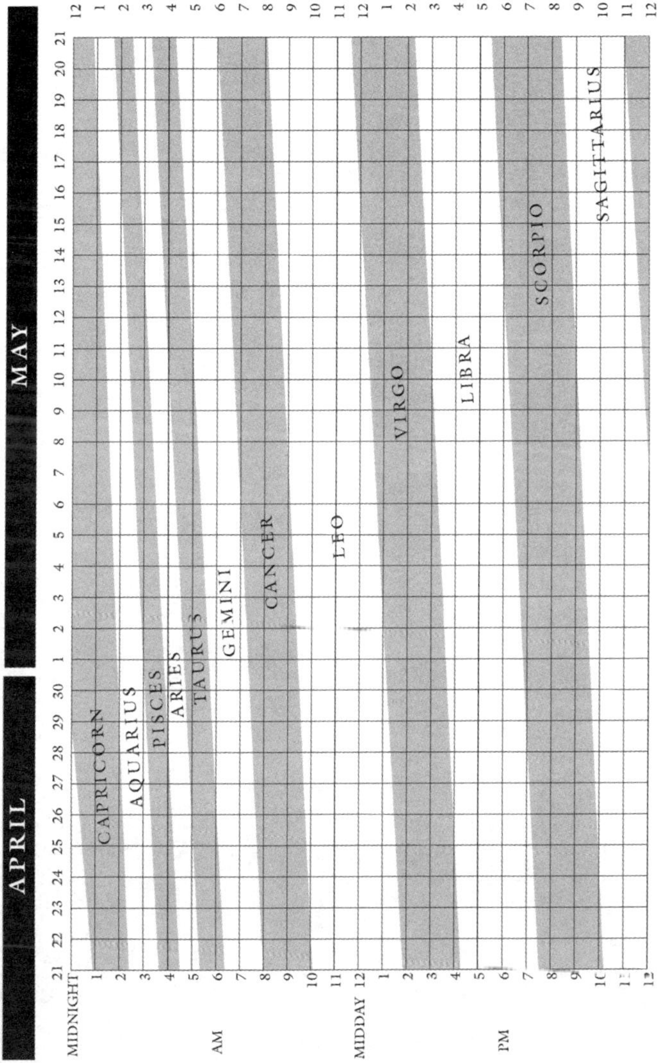

THE ZODIAC, PLANETS AND CORRESPONDENCES

The Earth revolves around the Sun once every calendar year, so when viewed from Earth the Sun appears in a different part of the sky as the year progresses. In astrology, these parts of the sky are divided into the signs of the zodiac and this means that the signs are organised in a circle. The circle begins with Aries and ends with Pisces.

Taking the zodiac sign as a starting point, astrologers then work with all the positions of planets, stars and many other factors to calculate horoscopes and birth charts and tell us what the stars have in store for us.

The table below shows the planets and Elements for each of the signs of the zodiac. Each sign belongs to one of the four Elements: Fire, Air, Earth or Water. Fire signs are creative and enthusiastic; Air signs are mentally active and thoughtful; Earth signs are constructive and practical; Water signs are emotional and have strong feelings.

It also shows the metals and gemstones associated with, or corresponding with, each sign. The correspondence is made when a metal or stone possesses properties that are held in common with a particular sign of the zodiac.

Finally, the table shows the opposite of each star sign – this is the opposite sign in the astrological circle.

Placed	Sign	Symbol	Element	Planet	Metal	Stone	Opposite
1	Aries	Ram	Fire	Mars	Iron	Bloodstone	Libra
2	Taurus	Bull	Earth	Venus	Copper	Sapphire	Scorpio
3	Gemini	Twins	Air	Mercury	Mercury	Tiger's Eye	Sagittarius
4	Cancer	Crab	Water	Moon	Silver	Pearl	Capricorn
5	Leo	Lion	Fire	Sun	Gold	Ruby	Aquarius
6	Virgo	Maiden	Earth	Mercury	Mercury	Sardonyx	Pisces
7	Libra	Scales	Air	Venus	Copper	Sapphire	Aries
8	Scorpio	Scorpion	Water	Pluto	Plutonium	Jasper	Taurus
9	Sagittarius	Archer	Fire	Jupiter	Tin	Topaz	Gemini
10	Capricorn	Goat	Earth	Saturn	Lead	Black Onyx	Cancer
11	Aquarius	Waterbearer	Air	Uranus	Uranium	Amethyst	Leo
12	Pisces	Fishes	Water	Neptune	Tin	Moonstone	Virgo